Well-Intentioned Advice

A life-voyage afloat

Jon Tucker

Also by Jon Tucker:

Snow Petrel (*a father-son voyage to the windiest place on earth*)

Also:

Those Snake Island Kids

Those Eco-Pirate Kids

Those Shipwreck Kids

Those Sugar-Barge Kids

Those Seal Rock Kids

First published in 2023 by Storm Bay Books

Copyright Jon Tucker 2023

This **Black & White** paperback ISBN: 978-0-6489157-7-5

Also as a Colour Paperback: ISBN: 978-0-6489157-6-8

Also available as an E-Book: ISBN: 978-0-6489157-5-1

For more information, visit **www.nzmaid.com**

Cover photograph: *New Zealand Maid in* d'Entrecasteaux Channel.

Author's note:

This is not specifically an autobiography. Please view it as a smorgasbord of bite-sized offerings which reflect the essence of an unconventional life-voyage. They are a mix of savoury and sweet, ready to be tasted according to your whim. I hope these may sate the appetites of all the readers who hungrily devoured *Snow Petrel* and requested a back-story.

Many of these pieces have previously appeared in maritime publications - in particular **The Marine Quarterly** edited by fellow-author Sam Llewellyn. It is largely due to Sam's regular prodding and quirky literary tastes that they came off the back-burner and into print.

The photographs which garnish many of these tales are largely due to the artistic eye of my life-long co-skipper Babs, without whom my life would have been far more ordinary.

Scorching up the Derwent under storm canvas in a force 11 blow, 1999

Exploring a creek en route to 'Duck Harbour', Waitara River, 2001

CONTENTS

Brief midwinter tranquillity in Paterson Inlet, Stewart Island, 2016

1

Well-Intentioned Advice
(and a dash of luck).

My life has been full of well-intentioned advice. Had I been sensible I might have heeded it and gathered wealth and security for my dotage. But from where Babs and I now contentedly sit, basking in the glow of our little woodstove aboard the gaff ketch that we call 'home', my single-minded obstinacy has nevertheless brought us a wealth of memorable pleasure.

"Build small," they advised. "Only a fool would build a yacht larger than 30 feet on a first attempt." Since my childhood, I had set my heart on building a 55 ft gaff schooner. So I compromised – more through the constraints of a small income than any acknowledgement of their good advice – and we settled on a 45ft Herreshoff ketch as our dream vessel.

"Don't build if you can't even afford the plans." Sensible advice indeed. The set of plans for our future ketch was priced at $250, a small fortune considering that my prospective salary as a novice teacher was to be a miserable $120 per week. We shrugged and borrowed the money, then waited impatiently for the blueprints to arrive – 17 wonderfully artistic drawings detailing even the subtle curves and scrolls to decorate the rudder, beak and trailboards.

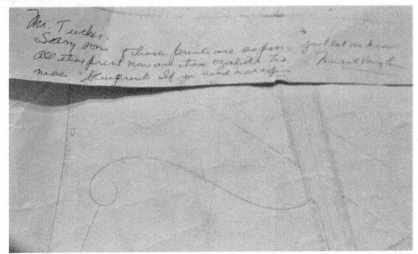

Blueprint detailing the rudder scroll-work, with Muriel's note.

Herreshoff had recently died, leaving his 'Marblehead Castle' dwelling and all design royalties to his housekeeper, Muriel Vaughn. The sheaf of drawings was accompanied by an encouraging letter from Muriel, so we pinned the line-drawing on the living-room wall of our little student flat and contemplated the next move.

"Build under cover." Impossible advice on my income. Finding a site was difficult enough. Luckily an aging farmhouse and acre at a token rental became available on the outskirts of Christchurch, complete with derelict outbuildings and an out-door privy, so we moved in and sought out demolition timber for the lofting platform and temporary station frames. We were in luck, as a nearby chicken farm was being dismantled, with timber for the taking. It was snowing by the time I was levelling the strongback in the back yard. The only cover for this build would be second-hand truck tarpaulins. Roll on summer!

With the advice against borrowing still ringing in our ears, we sold our beloved BSA 650, and lived frugally while the inverted hull took shape in the back yard. Petrol for our ancient Citroen was carefully rationed. Babs tended a vegetable garden with our first two boys in tow, and sewed

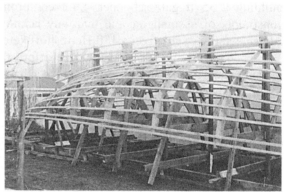

The hull takes shape, with stringers on frames.

most of our clothes. I moonlighted to supplement my teaching income, working nights in a hamburger bar and school holidays on building sites to afford the growing need for timber and fastenings. I cycled to school with a backpack weighted with student exercise books and half-deck beams to be shaped on the school bandsaw during lunch hours. We slept with the heady aroma of resorcinol glue wafting from various laminating jigs screwed to the bedroom floor. Babs balanced motherhood duties with a plethora of gluing and clamping tasks.

"Avoid teak decks. They leak!" This advice I ignored, convinced in my youthful wisdom that all traditional yachts should have laid decks. 'African teak' (iroko) was an affordable option so I doggedly persevered, adding four months to the build and decades of aesthetic satisfaction, regularly punctuated with the frustration of needing to re-caulk elusive leaking seams!

"Never go near a loan shark. They bite hard!" This advice sounded convincing, but we really-really-*really* wanted that nice new tractor engine at such bargain price! It was a hard lesson, especially when we later discovered the small-print penalising early repayments. Such is the naivety of youth.

This hard lesson was softened somewhat with a lucky tip-off about a pair of free masts. They had been sawn off a wrecked schooner five years earlier, and towed up a river where they apparently still lay on a stop-bank. The location was vague, and our chances seemed hopeless when we learned that the stop-bank had recently been raised by a couple of feet! It took a week's probing to discover and dig a fifty-foot trench to exhume the pair – both adze-hewn from solid fir trees and roughly clad in polyester resin. They were sufficiently serviceable to be stripped and modified, lasting for a decade until their heels rotted away – by which time our finances had allowed me to build the pair that still stand.

"You're so LUCKY!" We started hearing this comment regularly as soon as *New Zealand Maid* reached the water. We began to find it almost as irritating as the regular doses of Well-Intentioned Advice. Admittedly it is flattering to have an appreciative onlooker peering down at our lovely little ship, but having made a deliberate life-choice to sacrifice several years of comfort and free time on such a project, the inference that we lived a silver-lined existence was somewhat galling. By now we had three hungry young mouths to feed, and I was faced with a new job, four hundred exposed coastal miles away at Napier with an unrigged untested vessel to be motored north.

They say good luck can follow bad. Ten months before the launching, we had been mown down by a drunken truck-driver which failed to take the bend outside our gate walking home. It had taken several critical minutes for the paramedics to realise that much of the blood that splattered all three little boys was their mother's. My prolonged coma from a double skull fracture spared me the stress that Babs endured. The resultant good luck followed later in the form of a compensation payment which arrived in time to nearly cover the cost of the marine gearbox and propellor that was needed for the passage north.

Our luck did hold. The motoring passage to New Zealand's North Island was eventful but successful. We settled into a cheap schoolhouse pondering how to repay residual debts amounting to over half of my annual income.

Debt is burdensome. Babs wrote to all our creditors, assuring each of them that we could repay their credit at what seemed a rather pathetic monthly sum. Amazingly they all accepted. Meanwhile we dug another vegetable garden and I began shaping booms, gaffs and topmast out of redundant school rugby posts, given to us in return for a promise of running a sail-training club for interested college-boys. We began work on an interior temporary fit-out using demolition timbers. We borrowed sails and scratched together sufficient money for a gaff mainsail.

The first really big stroke of luck caught us totally by surprise. I was summoned from a sixth-form History class to take a phone call at the office. The film scout on the other end of the line sounded professionally genuine. He wanted our ketch for a significant movie featuring the replica of *Bounty*, with Anthony Hopkins as Bligh, and Mel Gibson as Fletcher Christian! We were to feature in the Portsmouth harbour scene (to be filmed in Gisborne) and the English Channel scene (near the white cliffs of Young Nick's Head). The payment offered was sufficient to cover all our remaining debt and buy a set of sails!

New Zealand Maid sandwiched between the other movie vessels, near the Bounty replica, in the 'Portsmouth loading' scene of The Bounty movie.

Being debt free opened many doors for us. With two more sons bringing our young crew total to five, we were now able to spend most school holidays living aboard and cruising. The older boys became proper little rig rats and useful crewmembers. When we trucked the boat home to our schoolhouse to build a cuddy cabin for'ard and a more permanent interior fit-out, the older boys busied themselves re-building a little fleet of black pirate dinghies for racing and camping.

Matt, Josh, Ben, Sam and Dan pose with their fleet of pirate dinghies: ***Dreadnought, Jolly Roger*** *and* ***Death'n Glory.***

More financial good luck was to follow. New Zealand was about to celebrate its 150th Jubilee and we were offered the role of a C19 trading ketch for a series of re-enactments in Wellington Harbour, participating alongside the Baltic ketches *Anna Kristina* and *Anna Rosa*. Babs and I were both restless once this heady action ceased, and with more money now in the cruising kitty it was time to move aboard permanently and take our chances without the security of a steady job.

The re-enactment of settlers landing in Wellington, with Maori 'waka' being paddled between ships. (Our ketch represented a very early trading vessel).

At this time the Well-Intentioned Advice burst forth once again. Advice against pulling our five boys out of classrooms and onto distance-education. Advice against sailing offshore and putting our youngsters at the mercy of the South Pacific. Advice against casting off the security of a steady income. We smiled politely, and continued the process of entering Babs as our skipper for the inaugural (and only ever) race through the Roaring Forties to the notorious Chatham Islands.

The pundits and sceptics went remarkably silent when the results were published. The fifteen-hour win on general handicap was certainly a feather in Babs' cap, and we spent three fascinating weeks cruising this remote small archipelago before returning to New Zealand and disappearing into the labyrinth of Marlborough Sounds waterways for the remainder of the year.

Sam learned to row as a 3-year-old.   *Ben, Dan and Josh at Awaroa, 1983*

There followed a pattern of stop-start 'lame seagull' cruising – a year or two of passage-making followed by a year or two on wages. The work came in many forms, from running a fishing ketch, delivering yachts, teaching, writing, boatbuilding, and house-building. Some might even say we were lucky having such a variety of opportunities to pursue our vagrant lifestyle. Perhaps they might be right.

The Well-Intentioned Advice reached fever pitch when we set sail to the French Nuclear Test site as part of a protest action. In particular our children's safety was under scrutiny. There may even have been whispers that we were we were lucky to return unscathed. Lucky? Hardly! For a venture like this one, the level of success is proportional to the level of planning.

One by one the boys left home. Or in some cases their home left them, as we cleared customs and left them on the dock. We moved into a new phase, cruising two-handed, unencumbered with extra mouths to feed.

There was definitely an element of luck that allowed us to stumble upon a few acres on a Tasmanian Island close by an excellent anchorage – especially as it was for sale at a credit-card price. The decade which saw us moored nearby while we built a rentable land base was punctuated by more ocean forays including to Antarctica, by which time the grandsons began arriving – six in total, with no sign of a girl! Cruising back in New Zealand again now with lively grandsons has added a new dimension to our cruising lifestyle. These lads have become useful rig-rats like their fathers and uncles, and our six-oared 12-foot tender has been as useful as it was a generation ago.

I imagine that during a future decade we will need to brace ourselves for another onslaught of Well-Intentioned Advice, urging us to consider moving ashore. Pah ... why on earth would we want to do such a thing? For us to follow that advice seems as unlikely as to have built a simple 30-footer!

But who knows....

***

New Zealand Maid with her original salvaged masts, Queen Charlotte Sound 1982. Our three little boys (aged 5.7 and 8) are rowing the gig back from an 'expedition'

Grandsons Nathan, Luke, Bradley rowing our 'longboat' with friends,2022

Grandsons Jeremy and Hadleigh exercising in our rigging Bay of Islands, NZ 2023

Grandson Loki enjoying a row in the gig near our Bruny Island property in Barnes Bay, Tasmania, 2022

2

'School trip' to the Chathams

Our first offshore passage aboard *New Zealand Maid* was an ocean race. Among the normal voyage provisioning was the boys' correspondence schoolwork. With five lively sons to cater for, two large boxes for each boy represented a lot of precious storage space. As parents, Babs and I were very aware of critical mutterings towards our decision to take the boys voyaging for an indefinite duration. However as trained teachers, we had no illusions about the necessity for conventional classroom-based education. Within a month our confidence was to be vindicated by a unique opportunity.

Our 450 mile route from Napier to the Chatham Islands, 1991

The Chatham Islands are a seldom visited small group of islands in the roaring forties about 450 nautical miles downwind of New Zealand's South Island. Vessels bound for Cape Horn seldom bother to drop in. The islands are generally shrouded in cloud, and offer only one dubious all-weather anchorage. Scattered near Pitt Island (the smaller of the populated pair) are a number of small rocky islets, barely accessible by boat. 'The Fort' and 'The Castle' derive their names from their topography, and the nearby Mangere Islet became famous overnight during the late 1980s with the discovery of three birds belonging to a species assumed to have become extinct several decades earlier – the Chatham Island black robin. One was an elderly female – soon to be named 'Old Blue', and her feathered companions were both males, one of which was later to be proven infertile.

From this precarious gene-pool bottleneck was to be developed arguably the world's most successful breeding exercise, bringing a species back from the most extreme brink of extinction. A team of ornithologists was assembled by NZ's Conservation Department, and the breeding pair was relocated to the slightly larger South East island half a mile south-east of Pitt Island. With them came some special recruits - a dozen similar-sized Tomtits which were to become surrogate parents for the ever-so-precious clutches of eggs produced by Old Blue and her single fertile partner.

Chatham Islands Black Robin

During the early 1990s, a small group of Kiwi yacht-racing enthusiasts came up with the idea of an ocean race which had never been attempted. The 'Inaugural Napier to Chatham Islands Race' was publicised throughout New Zealand, and at the peak of its promotion was hoped to field as many as fifty vessels in the line-up. However to put the concept in perspective, the Chatham Islands have a less-than enviable history of maritime loss of life. During the 1960s, a boom-and-bust crayfish frenzy saw large numbers of Kiwi coastal fishing boats attempting the Southern Ocean passage from NZ in casually arranged convoys. A significant number failed to arrive, and the resultant loss of life has cast a pall over these waters ever since.

New Zealand Maid may be a gaffer, but she is solid, seaworthy and no slug on a reach. A nice downwind race like this was too good to be true. With our five keen boys as crew along with Babs as skipper and my sister as bosun, we filled in the entry form and went about the business of meeting the NZYF safety criteria. One by one the anticipated ultra-light yachts pulled out. The finish-line, at Chatham Island's principal small settlement, Waitangi, is essentially an open roadstead with an occasionally usable big-ship pier and a few huge steel mooring-buoys. It was a no-brainer to deduce the unsuitability of the lightweight ground-tackle and removable anchor cleats aboard the thoroughbred race-yachts, for use in this destination. In addition, several applicants were declined on the grounds of skipper inexperience. The final line-up (rather to the chagrin of the organising committee) consisted of two cruiser-racers and our family-crewed gaff ketch.

*With a seabreeze at the start, off Napier's foreshore, **New Zealand Maid** carried a modest seven-sail wardrobe.*

As offshore races go, it was a fun passage. While the two favourites match-raced their way into a windless hole, we worked our southing on an overnight land-breeze, and rather gleefully invited the race-favourite's crew to an on-board barbecue late next day as we crossed tacks. Not surprisingly they declined.

Schoolwork was on the back-burner as we crowded on sail during the second day. To compensate for our lack of spinnaker, the boys managed to rig a total of ten sails, including tops'ls, two water-sails, mizzen stays'l and three heads'ls. Highlights for me were a partial solar eclipse and the joy of watching

The boys set a watersail under each boom

fifteen-year-old Ben calculate a star-fix, self-taught, within three miles of the position shown on our second-hand Satnav. Our 2200hr arrival at Waitangi in a force seven nor'wester, hooking up to one of the enormous steel buoys in a four-metre swell, revealed that we were only a few hours behind our rivals, and winner on general handicap by fifteen hours.

Next day, while the rival crews reputedly drank the only Waitangi pub dry of rum, we busied ourselves landing our unusual cargo through the surf at the most protected end of the beach. It was an awkward object to row ashore in our eight-foot dinghy, an emergency basket stretcher donated to the island by our local Lions service club. We had communicated with the island's sole police officer some weeks earlier while we were at the proposal stage for this gift back in central Hawkes Bay. In the flesh he proved to be a thoroughly personable cop, perfect for this island community. And he had something up his sleeve for us in return.

Clearly our visit could not have been timed better. For the first time since the black robin programme's inception - as a gesture of gratitude to the Chatham Island community - the conservation scientists stationed on South East Island were offering an 'open island' for locals over a three day period during the following week. In their own gesture of gratitude to us, the islands' emergency team was offering *New Zealand Maid's* crew the status of honorary Chatham Islanders.

There was a catch, however. Getting to South East Island was not a simple ferry ride. 'Ferry' is not part of the vocabulary in this part of the world. Travel here entails either climbing aboard a small plane to NZ, or hitching a ride on a fishing boat. Furthermore, the weather prognosis was clearly not looking good for the three days set aside for this opportunity. Over at Flowerpot (the Pitt Island haul-out beach for fishing vessels) the handful of crayboats were already retrieving all their pots before being dragged well above the HW mark for the immediate future. Meanwhile the three small Chatham Island fishing communities (Port Hutt, Kaingaroa and Owenga) had most of their fleets either high and dry or well tethered on their massive moorings.

Big swells and foul weather are a fact of life in these waters. (The compensation for local fishermen is that despite the many non-fishing days, there is usually an abundance of fish waiting to be caught on the good days.) It's a ninety-mile return trip between Waitangi and South East Island, doubling Cape L'Eveque, crossing Pitt Strait and rounding the south end of Pitt Island. The local lack of enthusiasm was hardly surprising. When our yacht showed up in the lee of South East Island on the final day of their three day invitation, our VHF call was met with a rather startled voice and a long wait, while we watched our depth-sounder fluctuating between 42 and 48 metres at seven second intervals.

Eventually a rather breathy voice came on air, explaining that the normal (tenuous) rocky landing beach on the eastern side of the island was unusable in this big swell. However, the voice continued, during the next hour a team of three would be attempting to launch an inflatable from the sheer rock face midway down our western side of the island.

I recently googled this island out of curiosity, in an attempt to understand the reason behind this choice of location. It is a scary satellite derived image, surrounded by a mass of white water, kelp forests and rock. The slab-sided nature of the cliffs and rock walls on the western shores are a stark reminder of the task which faced our brave hosts.

It seemed a long wait. Not surprisingly, the boys were excited. This would be a 'school field-trip' unlike any they had

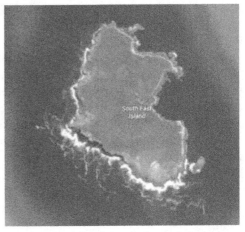

South-East Island (Rangitoto)

previously experienced. We discussed the logistics while we stood off, alternating between drifting downwind and motoring upwind. Clearly one of us would need to stay aboard and continue standing off while the others were ashore. A hasty lunch was eaten while Babs selected the warmest woollen gear to be worn under wet weather gear and lifejackets. Our adrenaline was up.

When one of the boys spotted three wet-suited figures inflating a zodiac on an exposed cliff-top, we motored closer and watched, intrigued. Huge kelp streamers sucked up and down the rock-face like writhing brown snakes. It seemed an alarmingly precarious exercise, and we held our breaths as the inflatable was hurled clumsily over the edge at the top of a swell, followed instantly by a wet-suited figure. Two more figures joined him on the next swell, seven seconds later, followed by some frenzied activity involving oars and a reluctant outboard motor. I caught Babs's eye briefly. Clearly, like me, she was hoping that these guys knew what they were doing!

The explanations came when the inflatable cruised alongside a short while later. Three tense but exhilarated biologists tossed us a painter and clambered aboard. Apparently nobody in the dozen-strong team on the island had expected a visitation on this final open-day, as the six metre swell made landing anywhere on the island virtually impossible. After our VHF call, these three had man-handled the zodiac for hundreds of metres across the island to the only obstacle-free location for the spectacular launching we had witnessed. The technique planned for our delivery approximated one used by traditional albatross nest-raiders on the local islets; nose up to a sheer rock-face and jump ashore at the top of a swell.

"Rule number one: aim to jump onto barnacles, not kelp!" directed the leader, eying our two youngest boys with a wry grin. "Two of us will be up there to grab your arms," he added, noting Babs' slightly ashen face.

It was to be a three-hour field-trip, with us adults arranging a switch in an hour or two. With no chance of anchoring here, one of us had to continue standing off aboard the boat. I watched apprehensively through binoculars as all six members of my immediate family made the wild landing during a succession of big swells. It was times like these that I was glad that we had encouraged our boys to climb trees and live an adventurous outdoor life. Babs was the last to land, stumbling slightly but recovering with apparent confidence. The wet-suited inflatable driver soon joined me aboard for a long wait and several cups of tea, as the landing party disappeared from sight.

The dedication of field-scientists like these is truly impressive. Tag-teaming with others from a pool of conservationists, they would spend upwards of two months at a stretch camped on this isolated island barely a mile long. Aboard our heaving yacht, between cups of tea, I gleaned a detailed picture of the black robin recovery programme. During five years of intensive hands-on nurturing, Old Blue and her boyfriends had been busily procreating despite the blanks fired by the dud male. There was now a population of nearly a hundred of their offspring on the island, and this was the first season in which the decision had been made to not interfere with the course of nature. Having spent several years handfeeding and nursing sick chicks, some members of the team were finding it heart-rending to simply observe any struggling young robins without intervening.

One issue from the tomtit surrogacy programme was an identity crisis, with some young robins attempting to behave like (and bond with) tomtits rather than their own species. Another concern for the team was the entire population's genetic identical vulnerability to a single disease or virus. The team would shortly be relocating small populations of breeding pairs to other islands in order to reduce the devastation of such a pandemic.

By the time my turn came to take the leap ashore, the tide had dropped somewhat, and the swells did not quite reach the top of the rock-face. I was certainly thankful for a pair of hands grasping my arm as I struggled to avoid the slippery kelp and gain a foot-hold. As I was led to the basecamp hut, I passed my own five exuberant offspring, accompanied by a pair of earnest young ornithologists, on their way to extract some of the fluffy young shearwaters for a weighing and tagging exercise.

It was mid-afternoon and mid-tide when the time came to re-embark. We had quite an audience this time, with several of our new-found friends accompanying us to the clifftop ostensibly to help recover the inflatable, but particularly to observe the spectacle. This time our instructions were to simply aim for the centre of the rubber craft below and jump exactly when told. Apart from a bruise or two this proved very successful, although one of the wet-suited team left his leap too late and missed the inflatable entirely.

None of our boys have grown up to become field-scientists, but all look back on their schoolwork afloat with appreciation. In particular they speak of the flexibility and variety throughout their childhood which they have carried into their adult lifestyles.

And not surprisingly they all now have yachts of their own.

***

New Zealand Maid shows off her traditional lines.

3

Schoolwork Afloat

New Zealand Maid was already down on her marks when we loaded the first year's correspondence schoolwork aboard - ten boxes in total, including copious workbooks as well as science kits, art supplies and even woodwork kits. With our youngest still at the pre-reading stage, and our eldest two already in their teens, we were taking a plunge into the unknown, and leaving our land-based existence behind.

Taking the kids and leaving our land-based existence behind.

Looking back on our subsequent semi-nomadic lifestyle, we have no regrets. We had a unique opportunity to connect with our children as a team, in an environment where even a ten-year old needed to be trusted to stand watch and keep us all safe. We had opportunities to sail to remote locations, meet isolated individuals, and face some truly daunting challenges. Our boys mixed easily with other children of different ages, cultures and languages, and communicated as comfortably with adults as they did with their peers.

Being teachers ourselves, we weren't particularly precious about the necessity of classroom-based education for our kids - children are programmed to learn (it is virtually impossible to prevent them learning) – we had chosen a *distance learning* option instead. But as we cast off from the constraints of suburbia, we were conscious of mutterings behind our backs. Some acquaintances even spoke their disapproval openly. In their eyes we were doing our children a disservice. How could the boys possibly succeed academically without remaining in a conventional learning environment?

We had cause to think of this a decade later, battling a November low-pressure system on our way back to New Zealand from New Caledonia. Matt and Sam had their important year 11 and 13 exams to sit a week later, and we had recently been dilly-dallying on an uninhabited island in the Loyalties with the kids camped ashore building rafts. Crunch-time was approaching. Would the critics be proven right? Years later, the proof is in the pudding, with Sam currently working towards his second degree, and Matt with three Antarctic expeditions under his belt, and a successful career-mix of film-making, building and Aviation rescue.

Dillydallying in the Loyalties before exams.

From a practical point of view, there isn't much room aboard a modest sized vessel for doing schoolwork. In our case, the saloon table was barely big enough for three of our five. Dan in particular - with his passion for artwork - found lack of space a challenge. However despite this he has become a successful artist/sculptor in adult life.

Schoolwork afloat is a topic of considerable discussion among parents who are agonising over whether to delay their voyaging until the kids have left home. For those, like us, who have chosen to pull our kids out of classrooms, there are decisions to be made about how best to cater for their long-term educational needs. Some choose the home-schooling option to varying degrees of success. We well remember a substantial American vessel which arrived in NZ with two home-schooled boys aboard, neither of whom could *hand-write* a legible word. Both parents had left successful careers in writing and computer programming behind, and had invested much personal energy into their sons' laptop-focused educational

Sam aged 12, doing schoolwork.

development, with particular emphasis on mathematics and science-related subjects. Their eldest boy then spent two finishing years in an exclusive NZ college, achieving Dux status.

But we know of other home-schoolers who have struggled, often through a lack of suitable resources and difficulties motivating their kids or structuring their daily routines. Pre-voyage preparations are difficult enough without having to research and locate suitable material for even a single child's year's learning. One tendency among home-schooling parents is to view the experiences of life afloat as a stand-alone form of education. While this has considerable validity, it doesn't address the issue of dealing with any future return to the NZ education system, with its curriculum-based achievement goals.

We have sailed in company with various overseas families during our voyaging, and been interested in the variety of options available to these parents. Sometimes an arrangement has simply been made with the children's school to provide a set of textbooks for use during a single year out of the system. Although this sounds a straightforward option, it requires considerable parental understanding of educational expectations, and can lead to difficulties even in areas such as modern maths which is taught very differently from the same subject a generation ago. For secondary aged students this is an even greater issue, with some subjects bearing little resemblance to those of their parents.

Some countries have a distance education option available, which reflects the education system of the country or state of their origin. Many of these are expensive, but they do have the advantage of potentially keeping their students in line with their cohorts.

New Zealand sailing children are the envy of many overseas sailing parents. They have the option of being enrolled (at no cost) at the NZ Correspondence School (Te Kura). This outstanding facility caters for all NZ school-aged children who are unable to attend a physical school. Any Kiwi kid who is sailing or road-tripping with relocations at least twice a term is classified as itinerant. All Kiwi children in non-English-speaking countries (or at sea) are classified as overseas students.

We were thrilled when our middle son Josh and his wife Sara decided to take the plunge themselves recently and sail around the world with three of our young grandsons. Having been a Te Kura student himself, Josh was quick to persuade Sara to utilise this wonderful NZ distance learning option. We were able to meet the two Te Kura teachers who were to be responsible for these three boys, and discuss how their teaching practices have evolved since our sons were learning through Te Kura. Between them they teach up to a dozen sailing kids at any given time, mixed into their 'classes' of nearly thirty students each.

Sam and Matt take time out from schoolwork during a tropical shower.

In our five sons' era, the year's schoolwork was laid out in eighteen sets of workbooks, with each set covering all subjects and roughly equating to a fortnight's work per set. It was up to us as parents to motivate and manage their time to complete these, and to return them for marking. Today there is a rather different approach, especially at Primary school level where the buzz phrase is *inquiry-based learning* – a flexible approach that we wholeheartedly agree with. For example, when we were running the tuna-fishing ketch *Sunniva* during the mid-nineties, one of the boys was faced with a science set about spiders. Babs was quick to re-write the exercises into an investigation of skipjack and albacore, allowing the same investigative outcome goals to be met. The teacher was delighted.

What immediately impressed us about our grandsons' two teachers was their commitment to getting their students motivated. Shortly before our grandsons left to go voyaging, we saw the delight on nine-year-old dinosaur-mad Nathan's face when he sneaked a look inside his box of schoolwork to find a T-rex cover on his first booklet. By tailoring workbooks to each student's personal interests the teachers are already forging a motivational relationship." This is vital for a successful family-cruising lifestyle. We well remember talking with an Australian parent who gave up cruising in despair after a continual battle trying to motivate an uncooperative youngster.

"Kids on boats are already in an amazing learning environment," explained Nathan's Te Kura teacher. "The flexible *enquiry learning* approach involves channelling them to learn about their immediate environment, formulating questions about the local geography, culture or even their oceanic surroundings. From these come genuine learning experiences which translate into maths and writing as they describe their findings." Her comment brings back a memory of our own, when our 15-year-old son Ben surprised us during the Chathams race by plotting a four-point star fix, *totally self-taught*. (He later left home at seventeen to study for his Foreign-going Mate's ticket in the UK, and now teaches navigation and shipboard safety.)

New Zealand's Te Kura also supplies a core of curriculum-based material to keep students up to a level comparable with their peer-group back in NZ. This covers reading, writing and literacy goals as well as appropriate numeracy and mathematics goals. This material used to be in the form of the workbooks with assessment sheets which were a challenge to send and receive from a voyaging vessel. Our youngest son, Matt spent half his school life being correspondence educated, and we have memories of packages missed in transit. Satellite coms were a rare option a decade or two ago, and we remember the thrill once of receiving exam results through a neighbouring yacht's HF radio link while anchored at an uninhabited island.

These days, it seems, technology has made the exercise somewhat easier. Internet wifi is available for uploads and downloads in many ports of call (and even aboard a growing number of yachts) so the exchanges are regularly possible via the web. Teachers can simply nominate specific pages of their workbooks and other assessable material to be sent as scans or even as mobile phone images.

This evening, as we write, another Facebook post arrives from Josh and Sara's 50ft *Rogue*, which is soon to cross the Atlantic. Josh is apologising for the lack of posts recently ("the Wi-Fi is pretty dodgy here!"). Our three grandsons have been snorkelling in crystal clear Mediterranean waters and exploring a thousand-year-old castle. One photo shows them at the saloon table, hunched thoughtfully over their workbooks. What an education they are having!

Grandsons Luke, Nathan and Bradley pore over schoolwork in **Rogue**'s *saloon.*

4

Tuna Trolling Under Sail.

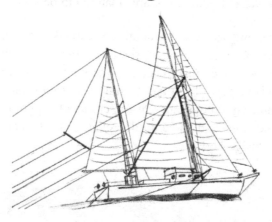

Sixty miles out from New Zealand's west coast, the Tasman Sea can be as unforgiving as the North Atlantic when the Lows roll in. Yesterday there were twenty fishing-boats trolling within a fifteen square mile area, but today all except ours have gone, diving for cover across Auckland's notorious Manukau bar before the rising swells close Auckland's little used west coast back door for an indeterminate duration.

Aboard the 48ft steel fishing ketch *Sunniva*, Colin and I have opted to ride this gale out. We are still towing eight of our thirteen tuna lures as the rising seas begin to sweep the aft deck. Colin chose to cut the engine – a 6LX Gardiner – an hour ago, bearing away when the nor-westerly rose above 25 knots, and we are now reaching under reefed main and stays'l. The disadvantage of trolling with a strong beam wind is that the nylon lines arc to leeward in our wake and the lures are prone to cross each other, becoming tangled in the white-capped turbulence astern.

'FISH' yells Colin as first one then three lines suddenly go bar-tight, zipping steeply downwards. The ensuing drill has become second nature by now, but as we hasten aft from the warmth of the wheelhouse, we are both aware of the need for caution on an exposed heeling deck swept with knee deep green water.

It is a profitable enough exercise, and within twenty minutes of vigorous action, nine good sized albacore tuna, ranging from six to eight kilograms, are sloshing among the melting ice in the slurry bin.

"That's enough," yells Colin, his Canadian accent barely audible above the multitude of noises which accompany any steel sailing vessel in a seaway. "I'll get the lines in while you ice these fish down. We're heaving-to till this blows out."

*

Sunniva was built in the late seventies as the fuel crisis began to bite. Designed by Dunedin naval architect John Hakker, she was New Zealand's first purpose-built sailing fishing boat for thirty-odd years. Ketch rigged with four roller-furling sails and a five-ton ice hold, she began life long-lining for gummy sharks - with a family trip to Tonga as a bonus for her first owner's wife and two kids. Evidence of that tropical voyage is still evident from my bunk in the focs'le, with the remnants of children's coloured comic stickers adorning the deck-head. When Colin Armstrong bought her in the early nineties, a refit including replacement of sections of the 5mm bottom plates of her hard-chine hull was necessary before beginning the next phase of her fishing career.

I had chanced upon Colin and his distinctive vessel during a yacht delivery in late 1994. My bread-and-butter career teaching History and Geography couldn't compete with his offer for me to join him for the December-March tuna season.

Sunniva was NZ's first purpose-built sailing fishing boat in three decades

Tuna trolling is unquestionably one of the most sustainable forms of commercial fishing in existence. Of the huge schools of pelagic albacore (and the less desirable skipjack), only a tiny percentage will successfully take a lure. Even when twenty boats are in a 'hotspot' (a locality where the fish have aggregated briefly) the bulk of the fish will live to see another year (unlike those caught in a seine net). New Zealand's so-called 'tuna fleet' in the nineties comprised an odd-ball mix of smallish cray-fishing boats, trawlers and longliners which had left their various local grounds for a month or three in search of a little adventure and camaraderie. Maybe forty in all, seldom over fifty feet in length, they could be found in small packs working a variety of locations at any given time during the season. The mentality and lingo mirrored the culture of old-time goldfields. They would head out 'prospecting', 'stake their claims' (and share their discoveries with only their closest mates), then 'set up camp' each night to lie on sea anchors in the ever-changing tuna locations.

Yet despite any rivalry, the HF 4417 mHz radio-frequency would be alive at night with catch figures and essential information about who intended to discharge their catch into whichever ports. Nobody wanted to be tied up for days in port waiting on a queue for ice supplies. And when anyone was in trouble there would always be plenty of offers for engine spares or even a tow.

*

It is now 40 hours since *Sunniva* was hove-to, and the day has dawned to a sullen grey sea, a mere fifteen knots of wind-slop on top of a three-metre groundswell. Sixty-odd miles away, inside Manukau harbour, twenty boat crews must by now be fretting in their wheelhouses, anxious for the swell at the entrance to ease sufficiently for the barway to be declared safe. Colin and I are stiff from the hours of 'dodging' at the height of the blow yesterday – hand-steering through large breaking seas in single hour watches with the deep-reefed main sheeted flat and the Gardner growling underneath the wheelhouse. It had been a relief to set a backed stays'l before dark and lash the helm down again as the weather perceptibly eased. Now with the prognosis of three better days, we are keen to get the lures back in.

Sunniva's yacht hull has given us a clear edge over our competitors. Breakfast over, we begin working our way southwards towards Cape Egmont, watching the sounder and thermometer and streaming our thirteen lures, brightly coloured this time, as is the norm for a dull day. We are the sole prospectors for now in this patch of the Tasman Sea.

*

The lure of gold is not dissimilar to the grip that this type of fishing has on an adventurous psyche. After my season of albacore fishing with Colin, returning to a temporary teaching position was somewhat anticlimactic. However within a few months, Babs and I were off on another adventure, sailing *New Zealand Maid* with three of our five sons on a 3000 mile midwinter downwind sleigh ride through the roaring forties from Wellington to Moruroa Atoll, as part of an informal international flotilla in protest against the resumption of French nuclear testing. The impending hurricane season eventually forced us back to New Zealand, and within days there was a call from Colin. He had agreed to deliver a 90ft fishing boat to Wellington from Japan. Babs had experienced three trips with us the previous year, and needless to say we both leapt at the chance to run *Sunniva* for the next three months.

And so, another season unfolded. This time there were four of us aboard, as our ten-year and twelve-year-old sons Sam and Matt were both more than happy to continue their correspondence education for another term with the bonus of pulling fish on the good days.

The lessons learnt from the previous season stood us in good stead. *Sunniva* could be sailed or motor-sailed to and from the fishing grounds, but streaming lures was best done under power. Dead upwind and dead downwind, a mile or two at a time, was the best way to tow lures – less chance of tangling lines or crossing paths with other boats in the locality. For most tuna boats with their distinctive poles, eight lures were the maximum. *Sunniva* was exceptional, able to stream thirteen lures thanks to her ketch rig. Two particularly long poles angled out to port and starboard from the mizzen chainplates, stayed to the lofty mast-head, with each one streaming three lines of dissimilar lengths. Another two short poles were stayed off the main chainplates, each supporting a five-metre surface lure as well as a downrigger which towed a short line two fathoms below our aft quarters. Two other downriggers angled steeply down from each side of the transom, and finally (in an ultimate nose-thumbing to the mere mortals of the fleet!) a thirty metre line streamed aft from the mizzen mast-head. No other boat on the tuna grounds could tow the number of lures as we did on *Sunniva*.

When it came to pulling fish aboard, we were almost as limited as the boats around us. Two hydraulic friction winches could do the donkey work pulling long lines while we hand-hauled the short ones. With our young crew as extras, it was possible to be bringing in six fish simultaneously. The reality, though, was that an average day might see around seventy or eighty fish in total, although our all-time record of two tonnes of 5 kg fish was the day's catch that could be off-handedly referred to as if it were the norm!

Sunniva's long tuna poles were suspended from her mizzen mast.

The albacore are certainly a fascinating fish. Their white flesh has a poultry-like texture when cooked, giving rise to the term 'Chicken of the Sea' in the US where its consumption far outstrips any other fish species.

Capable of incredible speed, their respiratory system requires a secondary 'booster' to keep their metabolism efficient. As a result, once caught, they will heat up steadily, contaminating their flesh with dangerous levels of histamines unless rapidly chilled in a slurry of ice and water. The not uncommon horror stories of entire catches being condemned on discharge kept most prudent skippers wary of the age-old 'fisherman's frenzy' which might see a ton or more tuna flapping on a sun-warmed deck as the crew continued to haul a 'full-house' of lines.

The strategy of 'prospecting' is an art in itself. Albacore are extremely sensitive to temperature variations, and can only be found in waters between 14 and 17 degrees Centigrade, unlike their cousins the skipjack and yellowfin which cope with somewhat warmer waters. Weekly satellite charts reveal the surface isotherms, which are the prospectors' first clues on likely locations for hotspots. Of particular interest are the thermal breaks where warmer water meets slightly cooler currents, akin to an aquatic cold front. Schools will mass behind these breaks, unwilling to venture into any water temperature outside their comfort zone. As the season progresses, the schools migrate southwards in synch with the surface temperatures down the west coast of New Zealand's South Island, then gradually northwards again.

Another valuable tool for the prospector is the 'bathy chart'; a map detailing the topographic contours (bathymetry) of the sea-bottom. Undersea peaks, canyons, trenches, plateaux and rises, all with their own local names, interact with ocean currents to generate upwellings of squid and other small-fry which are the feed of the ever-hungry schools of albacore. With its metabolic necessity to be continually on the move, each fish consumes around a quarter of its body weight each day.

Whenever a prospecting vessel strikes a 'hot-spot' her skipper is obligated to inform his best mates of the location. In so doing, he will have returned a similar favour or ensured a future one. However the airwaves have ears, and the manner of passing on confidential lat/long details could entail considerable ingenuity. Elaborate codes would often be developed between allied vessels, utilising obscure frequencies. Mobile phones (when in range) could be useful too. But with some rogue vessels becoming equipped with scanners, such airwave communications were never infallible. I well remember a particular vessel once steaming alongside, her skipper furtively holding up a battered oilskin displaying a simple set of lat/long numbers, before slipping discretely away to seaward.

Human nature being what it is, however, the location of a hotspot could seldom remain confidential for long. Due to a multitude of overlapping alliances, the details would become steadily disseminated across a hundred square miles, and within a dozen hours the hotspot could well find itself home to a score of diverse craft.

Early starts and busy evenings would be taken for granted aboard *Sunniva*, as indeed is the case on most fishing boats. 'Morning bite' and 'evening bite' on an albacore boat had nothing to do with breakfast or dinner. The terms referred to the greater likelihood for fish to take a lure as the light dimmed and sea surface cooled a little. Even our two boys revelled in the chance for extra action, after watching for the elusive green flash as the sun's upper limb disappeared over the horizon. Then, once darkness fell and mealtime was over there would be lines to retrieve and the business of making camp for the night.

The strategy of staying put for the night, some sixty-odd miles offshore, would vary from vessel to vessel. Some of the larger boats might simply set a parachute sea-anchor, flick on the radar alarm and turn in for the night. Others would launch less expensive drag devices, such as two or three fish bins bridled to the bow. Only the more vigilant might set anchor watches, or compromise like us with alternating lookout alarms set on the hour.

Aboard *Sunniva,* lying ahull under reefed main overnight was our most comfortable option to escape the sleep-defying roll of a twin-masted yacht without steadying sail. It was a judgement call to steam upwind for an agreed guesswork distance to compensate for overnight drift, sheet the main amidships, lash the helm down and turn on the mast-head strobe. Our strobe was not technically legal, but neither were anchor lights or navigation lights for a vessel under way but not under command. Overnight collisions were not unheard of either, and on a dark night a red or green light from a drifting vessel might not portray her actual direction of travel.

For Babs, as schoolteacher and first mate combined, the boys' schoolwork provided an extra dimension, with some of their land-focused worksheets needing modifying to allow for our marine environment. They became experts at measuring tuna instead of spiders.

*

The albacore schools which have survived the ravages of the Pacific seiners still migrate to the Tasman Sea during the Southern Hemisphere summer. But the New Zealand privately owned fishing-boat numbers have dwindled. Like so many parts of the world, the big New Zealand company-owned ex-Icelandic trawlers have shouldered the small operators aside. An entire snapper ground which would provide a 40ft long-liner with a sustainable season's worth of export quality fish can be cleaned out in two days by pair trawlers, the bycatch belly-up in their wake and the crushed snapper, from net cod-ends, fit for little else but fish fingers. The small harbours are now littered with abandoned mid-sized fishing vessels, their carvel planking as gapped as venetian blinds. The lucky ones have been resurrected as cruising boats. Only a handful of adventurous cray-fishers might occasionally be sighted offshore, prospecting in the hope of eking out their diminishing incomes with some low-priced albacore and skipjack catches.

And *Sunniva* survives too. Recently she could be seen in the trade-a-boat column, advertised as a sturdy potential cruising vessel – in need of a little TLC.

***

Dan holds an 8kg albacore, caught in the Pacific

5

Protest Voyage to Moruroa

Throughout my formative years, mention of the French nuclear test zone at Moruroa stirred many emotions. Like most Kiwis, anger and indignation were at the fore, particularly during the atmospheric testing phase when traces of radioactive *strontium 90* were found in our regular milk supplies. Such was the public and political backlash in 1973 when the French government defied a World Court injunction against atmospheric tests, that the NZ and Australian governments sent three frigates briefly to the test zone, carrying MPs from both New Zealand major parties as a symbolic gesture of protest. Meanwhile an equally significant handful of heroic private vessels made the epic voyage to defy the French navy's unilateral hundred-mile exclusion zone for months on end. To me, the crews of **Fri** and **Spirit of Peace** were true heroes whom I held in awe, even later when some became personal friends.

THIS two-masted boat made its message clear to the USS Wadsworth when the United States warship entered the Port of Napier for a three-day visit on Saturday. A small flotilla of boats and canoes protested peacefully.

With the cessation of atmospheric testing in 1975, Babs and I were more focused on the NZ Peace Squadron's civil disobedience activities, blockading Kiwi ports from any visiting nuclear warships. These were the heady days of the late seventies and early eighties, with hundreds of vessels, from kayaks to ketches, defying police cordons to bring nuclear armed or powered submarines, destroyers, and aircraft carriers to a shuddering halt at the harbour entrances of several major cities. Eventually the landslide election victory of the Lange Labour government in 1984 led to NZ's nuclear-free policy becoming enshrined into legislation which still survives.

When Greenpeace's *Rainbow Warrior* was blown up in Auckland Harbour by French secret agents seeking to deter her from protesting against Pacific nuclear testing in 1985, New Zealand was united in fury. In the public backlash against all things French, even champagne sales suffered. Nonetheless, underground tests at Moruroa atoll continued at intervals during the next five years, despite well-publicised evidence from Jacques Cousteau that *caesium 134* and *iodine 131* were leaking into surrounding waters. *Rainbow Warrior II* (bought by Greenpeace using French compensation money) also gathered evidence in 1990 that *caesium 134* was being carried by ocean currents well away from the test zone. At last, bowing to international pressure and an international moratorium, President Mitterand declared a halt to any further French tests.

So, when Jacques Chirac announced in 1995 that France would resume underground nuclear testing at Moruroa, a roar of angry disbelief rose from Oceania and Australasia. I still vividly remember Greenpeace's David McTaggart on NZ TV: '*I hope that the Kiwis, who are the best sailors in the world, get together all the boats they can and just wander over to Moruroa. You don't have to go inside the 12-mile zone, as even when you are outside the 12-mile limit they have to put a warship onto you and it bothers them. The more that can get there the better. Please come.*'

'Just wander over,' he said, talking about a winter Southern Pacific voyage of about 3000 nautical miles. This is equivalent to a North Atlantic crossing, well beyond the scope of most mortgage-bound boat-owners. Babs and I, though, had very few impediments. We were living aboard *New Zealand Maid* in a central Wellington marina, both on temporary teaching jobs with the kids on correspondence schooling. Lack of money was the biggest problem, although we were prepared to run up big debts if necessary. *New Zealand Maid* was a seaworthy boat, but we had to face concerns about exposing our children to the extraordinary hazards of such a venture.

Early estimates indicated that the flotilla might be over fifty strong. However the final number was fourteen, with nine vessels being from the country's north, including Auckland, and two from the South Island. In the middle, we were joined by two other yachts from our Wellington marina, where we formed a central New Zealand flotilla of our own, sharing the pressures of public scrutiny and fundraising as evenly as possible.

It was useful (and unique) that we had three protest flotilla vessels being prepared in our single marina. Our neighbours, Nick and Taff Gales with their two very young children lived aboard an Australian-flagged 54ft steel ketch, *Kela* . Our other near neighbour, Lynn Pistoll, was an Alaskan who had sailed his 42ft fibreglass sloop *Joie* to NZ fourteen years earlier. Lynn became enthusiastically involved when he noticed the serious activity surrounding *New Zealand Maid* and *Kela* a week after our decision to answer the call. His boat needed a total rig overhaul, which gobbled up a fair chunk of our small group-budget. In exchange, he made his office available as a coordination HQ, and even craned *Joie* aboard a low-loader to be parked outside the French Embassy one morning, surrounded by placard-wielding protesters.

Media attention was fierce but necessary, and the interruptions it caused took their toll on our schedules. A typical day began at 0600 with a radio station bringing microphones on to the ice-glazed decks. At 1030 the crews of all three boats would be chivvied on to *New Zealand Maid*'s foredeck for a newspaper photo. Four hours later the leader of the German Greens Party was swept aboard for a photo opportunity (we left our two youngest sons to deal with questions while we did urgent work on the engine). That evening Nick off *Kela* would be the chosen victim to face a live TV3 interview.

A list of several hundred hopeful volunteers, all claiming much sailing experience, was being circulated among the committed vessels. Nick selected four crew for *Kela* in the hope that it would relieve the pressure on him as skipper if things got tough. Babs and I had always voyaged with our five sons. But our eldest son Ben was studying for his foreign-going mate's ticket in the UK, and seventeen-year-old Josh was committed to the Royal NZ Yacht Squadron's youth sailing team. That left ten-year old Matt, twelve-year old Sam and nineteen-year-old Dan, who gave up his well-paid job in the fishing industry to rejoin us. So when Adriaan showed up unannounced on our dock with a recent square-rig North Atlantic crossing under his belt, offering to help us overhaul the rig before departure, we took him on immediately. A week later we chose Jim from the list, a mild-mannered fifty-year-old former fishing boat skipper turned Greenpeace driftnet diver. Our final 'crewmember' was mechanical - Charlie, a second-hand homebuilt servo-pendulum self-steering unit, who ate nothing except steering cables, for which he had an annoyingly voracious appetite.

There was a lot to do in the six weeks before our departure deadline. *New Zealand Maid* had been built in our back yard years earlier on a tight budget and we now needed to buy or borrow some expensive gear. This included an 8-person liferaft, longer range HF radio, Pacific charts, up-to-date flares, upgraded charging system and replacement battery-bank, almanacs, comprehensive first-aid kit, a new-fangled digital GPS, various rigging and engine spares, an extra water tank, and hopefully a drogue. It was a relief when offers of loan gear began to flood in: an eight-person life-raft freshly serviced, a powerful long-range HF radio and a GPS unit came in quick succession, greatly easing our budget nightmares.

For Babs there was the added burden of preparing provisioning lists for a three-month voyage of which over 90% would be spent at sea. Without a fridge or freezer, her options were more limited than those of most other vessels in the flotilla. We also needed wet-weather gear and thermal clothing, and to consider the children's schoolwork and potential medical needs.

Meanwhile, Pacific Peace Flotilla shore-based volunteers set up a headquarters in Auckland, arranging fundraising, logistical support, sponsorship deals and media reports. However there were no coordinated departure arrangements. All of the Kiwi yachts except our Wellington group cleared on different dates from a variety of ports, the earliest being a fortnight before us.

Two days before we sailed, five overflowing pallets of food arrived at Chaffers marina, to be shared among our little fleet. It felt like an early Christmas. By this time we had been joined by a fourth vessel, the brand-new well-found 54ft steel sloop *Chimera* from Greymouth harbour on the South Island's exposed west coast. Her owner, Gary, was a rookie skipper with an enthusiastic rookie crew, who had decided to sail in our company to compensate for his lack of voyaging experience. We were amused at his 120 cases of beer, but rather alarmed at his large-calibre rifle. It was a relief when Customs officers calmly took it away during clearance procedures. We were, after all, a Peace flotilla.

The departure itself was a bittersweet occasion. The media hype was exhilarating, but balanced by the emotion of parting with our remaining sons Josh and Ben, who had both flown in for a fortnight to help with preparations. Ben had stayed up all night on last-minute rigging work, and it was hard to drop him off onto a lonely

Our Wellington departure, heavily laden.

wharf at 0500hrs on the morning of his 21ˢᵗ birthday.

The first fortnight of the nineteen-day passage to Moruroa was a sleigh-ride down the Roaring Forties at their winter wildest. Front after front sped us on our way, always abaft the beam. Sometimes the greybeards were higher than our forty-foot-high mizzen mast. We were barely three days out when a sixty-knot gale had us all streaming drogues. *New Zealand Maid*'s engine flooded with seawater, which (despite our deck-high exhaust loop) backfilled the
cylinders. Our galley spoons still bear the scars of the difficult exercise of decompressing exhaust valves. But it had to be done. Without its alternator, our batteries would have been flat within days and our radios unusable.

Ten-year-old Matt stands his shortened helming watch as we run before a rising gale under trysail and reefed stays'l.

Balanced against the discomfort and perpetual damp was the camaraderie. It was common to have at least one other yacht in sight, and the VHF 'boardroom' discussions kept our little fleet connected. When Babs and Taff discovered that we had all the carrots and they had all the cabbages, we chose one of the steadier days for a close-range exchange. When *Chimera*'s freezer broke down we were pleased to swap some of our freshly-caught tuna for some rapidly thawing chicken.

On the thirteenth day we had sufficient easting to begin our climb north-eastward towards Moruroa. It was yet another vicious night. Lightning flashes revealed huge seas breaking on either side of the wake streaming away astern as we ran at six knots under only one tiny reefed stays'l. *Kela* was knocked down during the night, and her mainsail headboard was torn out. But the prospect of warmer latitudes ahead buoyed us through our watches.

Then the radio sched announced that the first nuclear blast had occurred. Riots were breaking out in Papeete, and the French military had confiscated *MV Greenpeace* and *Rainbow Warrior II*, Greenpeace's two largest vessels. Six other vessels including HMNZS *Tui* were already at the zone.

None of our four boats reached the variables unscathed. *Joie's* uncoupled propeller shaft disappeared out of the stern-tube and was replaced with a gush of seawater. Luckily it was salvable, but not without some heroic underwater activity. Then *Chimera* reported sluggish helming, and an exploratory dive revealed that all except one of her rudder flange bolts had disappeared.

The first puff of a southeasterly trade-wind was welcome. It was also a grim reminder that we were now nearing the Tuamoto archipelago, the region most affected by past and present French nuclear tests. On the same day we were 'welcomed', if that is the word, by the sudden startling scream of a low-flying French jet. We were being watched.

HMNZS **Tui** *greets us as we approach the prohibited zone.*

In the past, our landfalls had been characterised by the time-honoured 'Land ho' from a lookout aloft. Not so this time. We were still some sixteen miles short of our waypoint when a rather inelegant white ship hove into view and a Kiwi-accented voice crackled over the VHF. Almost before we knew it, a contingent of HMNZS *Tui*'s officers and crew were aboard each of our yachts, passing on a dizzying volume of information in a short space of time. An important part of this was an up-to-date chart of the twin islands of Moruroa and Fangataufa, corrected to WGS84 datum for our GPS sets. It had been a niggling worry that our ancient chart could inadvertently have set us inside the twelve-mile prohibited zone, where we could have been scooped up by a predatory frigate.

The NZ government had agreed to send HMNZS *Tui* shortly before we had left, in response to overwhelming public pressure for an official gesture of protest. At that point it had been made clear that although she would carry MPs, she would have no association with the flotilla. We now found out that due to public pressure, *Tui* had been authorised to provide logistical support to our Kiwi flotilla vessels, including refuelling, replenishing water tanks, and giving medical assistance.

And as for our biggest question, '*where do we meet the others?*' the answer was simple; '1.00pm, at the coffee shop.' This enigmatic location (21'40S, 139' 10W) was a point just over twelve miles SE of Moruroa's reef entrance, providing a marginal lee from the incessant trades, although not immune from the wraparound cross-swell (the legendary 'Moruroa Roll'), and beyond visual range of the low-lying atoll.

There could have been no better way to show national solidarity against the French nuclear test programme than our refuelling exercise next morning. With naval precision each of our four freshly arrived vessels took our turn to be refuelled courtesy of the NZ government, steaming on a course of 000degrees true at 4.0 knots, fifteen metres off *Tui*'s port quarter, under the indignant noses of two French warships. I spent a nerve-wracking half-hour at the helm, fighting

*Dan prepares to receive a fuel hose from **Tui***

the natural tendency for the two mismatched vessels to be sucked together, constantly aware that both the diesel and water hoses had a finite length which could not tolerate any significant variation in speed or distance.

This done, the two mothers, Babs and Taff, were whisked away with the kids for a dose of comfort aboard *Tui*, not to mention a solid dollop of media attention and a medical check-up. Meanwhile the rest of us had a flotilla meeting at the coffee-shop to attend.

*

We have often been asked how we kept ourselves sane during the next two weeks of busily going nowhere. One of the key sanity-savers was the daily strategy meeting at the coffee shop. These were an initiative of Greenpeace, who were an entity distinct from the rest of the Pacific Peace Flotilla. Their veteran campaigners were the most experienced activists amongst us, and certainly the best resourced. Though they had already lost their two flagships, Greenpeace still had the 90ft chartered schooner *Manutea* and their veteran anti-nuclear yacht *Vega* keeping station among the constantly changing flotilla vessels. David McTaggart was deemed to be the godfather, and on that first meeting, held aboard the big Kiwi topsail schooner *R Tucker Thompson*, I was impressed by his quiet authority.

The philosophy was simple enough: plan regular activities to frustrate the French whilst giving us a sense of purpose. The activities varied, but certainly helped structure the flotilla. All locations would be referenced to our Flotilla 'roadmap', a basic chart of Moruroa overlaid with Wellington city streets to prevent the mentioning of lat/long waypoints on the VHF. That first afternoon's rather crude action was for all ten boats to assemble in Taranaki Street and simultaneously rush the line on a coded command, ignoring any French warnings and not sheering away until the very last minute. This action brought two frigates, two patrol vessels and a helicopter rapidly on to the scene, accompanied by several tense and heavily accented radio voices attempting to identify and reprimand each vessel individually. The Chilean single-hander on *Bebinka* was badly knocked down by helicopter downwash, and the Kiwi yacht *Photina* missed his cue altogether, attempting to fix his position by sextant in the absence of a GPS aboard.

Shortly afterwards a zodiac roared alongside, manned by a group of armed marines delivering a polite but firm message from Vice-Admiral Euverte. This spelled out the official French definition of international maritime law, especially in relation to their suspension of the right of free passage between Moruroa and Fangataufa atolls. It stated that if we attempted to circumnavigate Moruroa, we would be venturing within twelve miles of the neighbouring atoll, and liable for prosecution. We declined their request to board us, on the grounds that they were carrying weapons in international waters. In return we handed them a carefully worded letter stating our view that France was abusing its political authority by overriding the wishes of all Pacific nations and creating a long-term contamination problem.

Days passed. The wind eased temporarily to a balmy five knots, and enabled safe socialising between boats and some cautious swimming. Some left, others arrived. The boys sent off a set of completed schoolwork to *Tui* before her departure to Rarotonga.

Some of our scattered fleet, barely visible in a typical swell while hove-to at the 'Coffee Shop' during a skippers' meeting aboard **R Tucker Thompson** *(foreground)*

The daily meetings became a ritual with *Vega*'s inflatable 'taxi' collecting skippers and various crew to meet aboard one of the biggest vessels. One action entailed an early morning 'huddle' whereby every available vessel came as close together as practicable to enable a canoe to be launched from an unidentifiable boat, and paddled ashore under the radar by a pair of dissident Tahitians. Another action required each of us to heave-to at specific waypoints scattered around the perimeters of Moruroa and neighbouring Fangataufa atolls, all rushing the line simultaneously at a predetermined time. This was not as pointless as it may seem – another blast was imminent on one of the two islands, and this was an attempt to work out which location was under the tightest military cordon.

Despite the camaraderie, the constant struggle to hold station against often strong trade-winds took its toll. Aboard *Kela*, one crewmember crushed two fingers while handing the sea anchor, and Nick made the understandable decision to cut and run for Papeete. Meanwhile we broke the boom of *New Zealand Maid*'s gaff mizzen and were forced to set the trysail as our mizzen, with the gaff spar as a boom. Chafe was causing trouble thanks to the incessant hove-to roll. The engine developed an overheating problem. Then Sam became unwell. The fleet had dwindled to five, although three more were shortly to arrive from New Zealand, Denmark and Germany. It was time to sail for Papeete, six hundred miles downwind.

It was a pleasant five-day downwind passage to Tahiti, but two surprises were waiting for us. The first occurred at a cash machine, which told us that *le solde de votre carte est insuffisant*. Despite my limited French, the meaning was plain. We were in dire financial straits, nearly out of fuel and fresh food, with 3000 miles to sail home.

The second was more complicated. Visiting the heavily bugged but furiously active Greenpeace headquarters on the Papeete waterfront, we learned that during the past few days both *Manutea* and *Vega* had been seized. Greenpeace desperately needed a vessel to convey a radio operator and their US head of operations back to the zone. Would we be prepared to sail *New Zealand Maid* back to Moruroa as the temporary sole Greenpeace representative vessel and hold station there until their latest replacement, *Caramba*, could be readied?

Babs was not averse to the notion, but was concerned about Sam's slow recovery. It was decided that Greenpeace would accommodate Babs and the two boys in a campground hut on Moorea, pay for our mizzen-boom repair and refuel us. The work was done swiftly, and we sailed without delay.

Gaff ketches don't like windward work. It was a six-day motor-sailing slog back to the zone into the teeth of the accelerated trades, with only Dan and Jim to share the burden of watch-keeping. By the time we arrived at a now-deserted coffee-shop our fuel tanks were nearly empty, and the French were clearly not amused to see us back. This was to be a lonely vigil, constantly shadowed by at least one frigate, maintaining a thirty-mile reaching track back and forth just outside the prohibited line. In our novel role as a satellite communication vessel, we balanced the big flat antenna on our knees pointing at the geo-stationary satellite thousands of miles overhead while a borrowed generator hummed and the reports were beamed skyward.

As skipper I now regret not knowing what some of these messages contained. Certainly they must have been provocative, for our naval 'escorts' became noticeably more aggressive. Clearly their officers disliked our banner too: *Le jour de honte est arrive,* a play on the national anthem, substituting 'shame' for 'glory'. To rub salt into the wound we also reversed the signal flag 'T' to create the red/white/blue French flag, including it in the message *honte*, which we displayed from our starboard spreaders. It was immediately noticeable that approaching warships would sheer away to pass on our port side.

Our banner and flag message clearly upset the French officers and crew.

On one notable occasion an especially aggressive frigate steamed very close alongside, with armed marines loaded into zodiacs hanging from davits. *Tui* was no longer in the area, and we felt particularly vulnerable, but held our course with the long-range HF radio warmed up in case of an incident. On our return I learned that Greenpeace had issued a media release to the effect that we had successfully launched a mini-sub. In addition, Babs was being unwittingly used as their propaganda conduit by being fed misinformation on the bugged HQ telephone. It is possible that *New Zealand Maid*'s name may have been our saving grace. As a Greenpeace representative vessel we were potentially vulnerable, but as a vessel bearing the name of a Pacific nation, any significant aggression towards us would be likely to create a media frenzy.

*The Frigate **La Nivose** constantly shadowed us.*

Sailing up and down the same track became decidedly tedious. Once we had the news that *Caramba* was on her way, accompanied by our old friend *Joie*, we seized the opportunity to slip away into a rare dusk when no frigate was visible. This enabled us to transfer Greenpeace's equipment outside French surveillance, and to land their representatives back at

Papeete. This was done under cover of darkness, as I had been belatedly informed that both their visas had been revoked, rendering me (as skipper) potentially liable for smuggling illegal aliens.

Occasionally we are asked whether this flotilla really made a difference. Well, a total of 32 vessels from twelve nations participated, maintaining a constant stream of media reports. It would be presumptuous to overlook the significance of the many parallel land-based protest activities, or the fact that this was Greenpeace's most expensive campaign ever. But the outcome was one we had all worked towards. The planned series of eight blasts was terminated prematurely, and within months Jacques Chirac announced that France would dismantle its nuclear testing infrastructure at Moruroa and sign a zero-threshold Comprehensive Test Ban Treaty (CTBT) at the UN, as well as the South Pacific Nuclear Free Zone Treaty.

There will always be vital issues which need public scrutiny, and waterborne protest action has been proven to be a powerful magnet for media attention. With the planet's oceans under increasing pressure for resource plundering and waste dumping, the United Nations Convention of the Law of the Sea remains a vital code to safeguard the rights of motivated individuals who carry out peaceful protest in international waters. Let us all hope that such rights survive, in an era of a fracturing world order.

***

"Just wander over..." said McTaggart. Yeah, right !

Letter to 'Monsieur le Skipper' from Admiral Euverte

FORCES MARITIMES
ET ZONE MARITIME DU PACIFIQUE

Papeete le 23/8/95

L'AMIRAL

Monsieur le Skiper,

You came, with your crew, to protest by your presence on board a sailing ship in the vicinity of the Mururoa atoll against the decision made by France to carry out a final series of 8 nuclear tests - due to end by 31 May 1996 latest - prior to signing the Nuclear Test Ban Treaty in 1996.

Naturally, I do not share your point of view, although you should know that I respect it. As long as your ship will remain on the high seas, no objection can be raised to your demonstration.

On the other hand, as you are a seasoned sailor, you must be acquainted with the rules of international maritime law pertaining to the right of passage of ships in territorial waters of a country whose flag they do not fly, and you must surely be aware that a coastal State has - pursuant to Article 25 of the United Nations Convention on the Law of the Sea (which reflects the common law pertaining to this issue) - the right to suspend locally, in specified areas of its territorial sea, the exercising of the right of innocent passage.

By the order n° 707 of 23 June 1995, the High Commissioner of the Republic in French Polynesia has suspended until 31 May 1996 the right of innocent passage in the territorial waters bordering the Mururoa and Fangataufa atolls. This measure is in conformity with international law.

If you contravene this prohibition, you will be liable to prosecution under French law which, as you know, is sovereign in this area.

The right of passage to wich your are entitled in the rest of th French territorial sea in Polynesia must therefore be exercised in accordance with international law and French regulations partaining to defense issues and to coastal security. Any infringement of French regulations will entail criminal prosecution.

As a sailor, I have spent a great part of my life at sea, partly in the Pacific, and I know that conditions can often be tough there. I assure you that I shall always react as a sailor should you encounter difficulties and that I would note hesitate to lend you assitance if necessary, but please also bear in mind that I am quite determined to enforce the law and to carry out the mission I hold to safeguard the security of the testing sites in order to implement the decisions made by the President of the French Republic.

Sincerely

Vice-admiral Philippe EUVERTE

Our letter to the Admiral

New Zealand Maid

TO: COMMANDER FRENCH MILITARY FORCES
MORUROA / FANGATAUFA.

We, owners and crew of New Zealand registered ship "New Zealand Maid", wish to inform the French government through you that:

a) We do not recognise France's right to create and contain nuclear wastes in the Pacific region against the wishes of nearly all Pacific inhabitants.

b) We do not recognise France's right to declare an exclusion zone around Moruroa and Fangataufa atolls.

c) In view of the French military's record of violence against peaceful protest we do not intend to endanger our children aboard this vessel by sailing inside the zone.

d) We feel strongly that France has abused its political authority by overriding the wishes of all Pacific nations and creating a long term contamination problem.

e) We are not anti-French, We admire many French citizens especially sailors like Eric Tabarly, Bernard Moitessier and especially Jacques Cousteau. However uniformed French military personnel are not welcome aboard this boat.

f) We are proving to Jacques Chirac that Moruroa is within easy access to ordinary New Zealand families and is part of New Zealand's 'back yard'.

Signed 10/9/95

J.Tucker

Don Tucker (owner skipper) New Zealander
Barbara Tucker (part owner) New Zealander
Daniel Tucker   New Zealander
Sam Tucker (aged 12 years) New Zealander
Matthew Tucker (aged 10 years) New Zealander
Jim McArthur   New Zealander
Adriaan Stroes   European citizen

6

Husbanding Sleep at Sea

I discovered an uncharted island once. It was shortly after launching *New Zealand Maid*, back in the days when the sky wasn't littered with satellites, and when hand-steering by compass was the norm on dead-reckoning passages like this one.

It had been a challenging sixty hours, beating our way across a huge bight, a hundred-odd miles offshore. With two water-spout sightings, and both mastheads glowing with St Elmo's fire during the second night, sleep had been virtually impossible. By this third night I was utterly drained and beginning to have serious doubts about the reliability of my course and position. To my befuddled reasoning, the ship which crossed our path shortly after midnight must surely have been bound for the same destination as ours. Navigation would now be simple, although a serious course alteration would be essential to follow its track, as our compass had obviously developed a startlingly big deviation.

At dawn, broad off the starboard bow, the distinct silhouette of a steep-sided island stood sharply against a pale grey horizon where my charted position showed nothing but open sea.

Don't be a donkey!" exclaimed Babs when she emerged from below-decks where our three young children were clamouring for breakfast. "Uncharted island? Not possible! Show me the chart." She was right of course. With her clear head, the adjusted course *as plotted* bore little relation to our actual track. This island was exactly where it was supposed to be, and a sweep of the dividers from my 0100hr dead-reckoning plot showed just how impaired my sleep-deprived judgement had become. It was a salutary lesson on how critical sleep management is on passage, and one which I have carried with me during the subsequent decades at sea.

"You need to *husband* your sleep!" This wise advice came a decade later from Colin Armstrong, the Canadian skipper of the tuna fishing ketch *Sunniva*. With just the two of us at sea for up to ten long days at a stretch, we needed to be capable of remaining adequately alert at night as we drifted hove-to amongst the Tasman Sea tuna fleet. During the potentially quiet afternoons when the heated sea surface discouraged the albacore from rising to our lures, we would take turns to catnap. 'Power-naps' we called them, twenty or thirty minutes of very deep micro-sleeps which would help compensate for the broken nights ahead.

Much has been written on the science of sleep. Aboard *Northern Light*, our friends Rolf and Debra have spent years managing sleep in high latitudes. Our son Ben is a strong advocate of their approach to sleep, condensing it into a nutshell. "Think of your sleep like money in your bank," he reasons in his *snowpetrelsailing* blog on storm tactics. "You put hours into it and you take hours out. Simple. And you do have an overdraft facility, but if you go too far into debt you'll be in serious strife. You particularly need to get plenty of sleep credits into that bank ahead of bad weather as part of your preparation - equally as important as shortening sail in advance and dogging the hatches. It'll give you a better chance of making rational decisions when the sh** hits the fan."

It is not just heavy weather that calls for the discipline of sleep management aboard short-handed vessels. Working our way through seemingly endless Antarctic pack ice aboard Ben's *Snow Petrel* we reluctantly took turns to power-nap below deck, despite the temptation to revel in the unprecedented excitement, knowing of the need for clear heads and effective lookouts.

Other experienced short-handed sailors, like *Hugo Boss*'s Alex Thompson, prefer the analogy of fuel in the tank. "I've slept five hours in the last three days and in the last 24 hours I haven't slept at all. I'm running on empty and looking forward to some sleep!" was his wry understatement as he swept towards his second-place finish in the 2016 Vendee Globe.

Alex clearly had a better handle on sleep management than many other solo sailors over the years. During the same year as my Uncharted Island Incident, one of my then-heroes, Kiwi solo sailor Dick McBride, fell more seriously victim to sleep deprivation during the 1982 inaugural BOC solo Round the World yacht race aboard his steel schooner *City of Dunedin*. In his case it was his inability to awaken from the deep sleep of exhaustion which spelled his near demise. He had successfully turned left at the Horn and was steadily working north into the Atlantic. Much of the day had been spent aloft repairing his twin forestays, and he was exhausted, setting his windvane to pass south of the Falklands before collapsing into his bunk for a nap. If he had left a little reserve sleep in his bank he might have been woken by the untimely

Dick McBride's sketch of rounding the Horn

90 degree wind-shift, but instead it was the crunch as he fetched up on a rocky beach that brought him abruptly to his senses.

Dick's outcome was more successful than some of his fellow competitors. Of the seven who failed to finish, three were sunk or wrecked. His decision to race in a heavy steel boat paid off, and after three weeks of pounding, *City of Dunedin* was eventually floated off and repaired in Stanley, allowing him to complete the race at the back of the fleet.

Decades later we were moored in Tasmania when a would-be solo circumnavigator abandoned his ambitions at an unexpectedly early phase of his voyage. I had first met Tony at Port Arthur in 1999 when he dropped anchor nearby and invited us aboard his gorgeous 36 ft wooden double-ender. He had devoted a decade of his life to building this impeccable vessel, and he had nearly completed his maiden (and only ever) solo voyage, day-hopping south to Hobart from Adelaide. The following five years were focused on preparing for his life-dream, a solo non-stop circumnavigation. Our son Ben had often suggested a trial shakedown offshore passage, but Tony was always far too pre-occupied with the more important task of readying his vessel. As his departure drew near, a score of local ladies busied themselves baking their best cake recipes, destined to be consumed and judged as his voyage progressed. Finally the big day arrived, with many of us hung-over from his farewell party while media helicopters hovered overhead as he set off triumphantly down the Derwent.

Three days later we heard his voice on our short-range VHF, preparing to dock in our modest Kettering marina once again. It had been a hard lesson for Tony, learning that he was utterly incapable of allowing himself to sleep under way. His ignominious decision to abort was a brave one of course, with a lot of humble pie to eat. What became of the cakes I never heard.

I have often wondered whether humans might train their brains to sleep like whales or dolphins. We regularly encounter *logging* whales progressing steadily on a constant heading in a semi-conscious state. Their left eye maintains lookout for twenty minutes while their right brain sleeps, then vice versa. This behaviour is actually a biological necessity for whale calves to avoid drowning, as they must slipstream in their mothers' wake for their first weeks (an *echelon formation*) until they accumulate sufficient blubber for independent buoyancy.

Another of my Kiwi heroes, Shackleton's captain and navigator Frank Worsley, displayed a similar condition during the epic *James Caird* small boat voyage to South Georgia. He recounts in his diary how he helmed throughout a horrendous Southern Ocean gale in a semi-conscious state, until eventually his unresponsive fingers were prised from the tiller by fellow crewmembers. Our son Josh is also capable of achieving this trance-like state. On one such significant occasion he continuously helmed for eighteen hours under storm spinnaker aboard the 9.2 metre *Pepe* in a two-man Round North Island race, afterwards having no recollection of specific occurrences for much of the leg. His teenage crewman later described coming on deck to find Josh as unresponsive as a sleep-walker. "But I knew that I couldn't drive *Pepe* anywhere near as well as Josh in those conditions, so I just sat with him a while then went back to my bunk and left him to it!"

I have a small scar above my left eyebrow resulting from a battle between my willpower and the inevitability of sleep. I had been struggling for hours to remain conscious, watchkeeping alone in a comfortable wheelhouse while the autopilot hummed and the minutes ticked towards a grey dawn. Intermittent doses of coffee were no longer effective, so I had resorted to remaining on my feet, swaying to the rhythm of the Tasman Sea swells as a safeguard against dozing. It was the sharp pain as my nodding head connected with the corner of radar screen, and the sticky redness of oozing blood that brought me to my senses. I have never since allowed myself to be locked into watchkeeping routines which compromise sensible sleep recovery.

Solo sailors under way are technically in breach of international collision regulations (ColRegs), relying on a variety of alarms to replace eyeball watch-keeping. This carries the responsibility of remaining capable of waking to these alerts, hence the need for sleep management. For hard-core racers this is a challenge. For softer sailors like Babs and me there is a simpler option. *New Zealand Maid* is a long-keeled Herreshoff with the ability to heave-to happily in most conditions. Babs and I have made the most of this practice over the years, sometimes to simply enjoy a comfortable meal, but particularly to take a break for sleep during heavy weather when there is adequate sea-room. We once listened in fascination to the nightly HF scheds of an unseen solo 'gentleman sailor' whose routine, as he trundled his schooner through the Pacific trades, involved heaving-to at nightfall and setting riding lights, then getting underway each dawn after a good night's sleep. On the other side of the spectrum, the arrogance of one reckless skipper recently raised serious concerns among other cruising sailors who were also returning to New Zealand ahead of the hurricane season. His was a large steel ketch with an AIS transmitter which he considered adequate warning for any nearby vessels to keep clear of his careering *unlit* vessel while he slept through the night on auto-pilot.

Slocum's solo sailing experiences of a 'companion' aboard during times of duress are mirrored by Tristan Jones' accounts of inexplicable visitations. Such experiences are generally gathered into the general category of sleep-deprived hallucinations. My strongest personal hallucination experience manifested in a very different manner, and seemed equally real at the time, back in the days when the tyranny of the helm dominated our short-handed passage-making. It was the third night of a frustrating windward passage, and I was struggling to reach the end of an extended moonless night watch. Gradually I became convinced that *New Zealand Maid* was somehow losing altitude. Instead of rising to each approaching swell, and sliding into the following trough, any sense of lift had disappeared. The sea had become a downwards staircase, each swell taking us steadily forward then downward, forward then downward.... It was sufficiently vivid to know that this was not a dream. I was still consciously helming on the correct course, capable of inspecting the sails by torchlight while all the while we seemed to be steadily descending towards Davey Jones' Locker. My determination to see out the watch dissolved, and I pulled the cord attached to Babs's ankle to bring some sanity back into the cockpit.

Perhaps the last word on the subject comes from the STCW shipping regulations regarding sleep for officers of the watch. After laying down stipulations for ten hours' minimum rest for any 24-hour period, including one of at least six hours, it immediately allows these to be ignored whenever necessary: *The requirements for rest periods need not be maintained in the case of an emergency drill or in other overriding operational conditions.*

Ha! *Overriding operational conditions!* These are the challenges faced daily by short-handed sailors. Wouldn't we just love a day with six hours of continuous sleep. Perhaps it's time to join the merchant navy and cross oceans in comfort.

***

Ben, exhausted in his quarter-berth during **Snow Petrel's** *voyage south.*

7

Undersized shipmates

Arthur Ransome's fictional feeble kitten *Sinbad* captured generations of young hearts, when he was scooped from a floating crate in the North Sea in *We Didn't Mean To Go To Sea*. Fiction often parallels fact, and during our years of wandering oceans, we have met many a ship's cat which has managed to endear itself to a boating family as a scrawny waif, mewing feebly on the dockside. Each one is a tale in itself but not all with happy endings, as their nine lives tend to be used up rapidly with each bout of heavy weather, especially given their pre-programmed inclination to balance on daringly narrow surfaces.

For vessels going foreign, pets are renowned for adding an extra layer of red tape, particularly at ports of entry. Quarantine officials are inclined to scrutinise a skipper who has declared the presence of any creature aboard. In an age of enhanced biosecurity, no matter how pampered a pet may be, it will still be viewed as an agent for the spread of disease or micro-organisms.

We vividly recall a large American launch which steamed into Wellington harbour with a well-fed family moggie reclining comfortably aboard. New Zealand regulations for such animals at the time required either their removal to a quarantine facility for six months, or the expensive alternative of a weekly inspection by an official (a choice which they took despite the thousand-dollar monthly bill). Immigration complications intervened shortly before the completion of this process, and the vessel was required to leave the country for an interval. On its return the entire process recommenced from scratch, and at last, six months later, the big day arrived for a 'coming clean' party. As the entire local live-aboard community gathered on the dock, we learned that poor moggie had died only a few hours earlier. Undeterred, we all enjoyed our on-board wake for the most expensive pet that most of us had ever encountered.

With five enthusiastic boys living aboard *New Zealand Maid*, it was inevitable that the occasional prospective pet would be occasionally smuggled aboard. 'Ducky Tucker' was only a tiny duckling when he first gave himself away with a plaintiff peep, snuggled inside Josh's singlet. Our token parental resistance stood no show against the combined pressure from offspring of various ages. Ducks are messy pets, but once the issue of excrement management had been negotiated, he became a popular little pet until he grew to reveal his drake feathers and an extraordinarily bossy temperament. There were no tears shed, months later, when he was 'actively encouraged' to stay ashore with his girlfriend (a paradise duck twice his size), frequenting a slipway where he became a legend, dining on antifouling residue and barnacles. Several years later we learned that he had been regularly spared from becoming a Sunday roast because of his presumed toxicity levels, and consequently grew to an advanced, rather cranky, age.

We once rather rashly bent to pressure and allowed a pup to become part of our crew. Like cats, any dog will ring alarm bells for quarantine officials, but we were not contemplating overseas voyaging at the time, so Bosun established himself as an alpha member of the crew. The wooden cleats were the first to suffer as he cut his teeth on any protrusion, and when the eight-spoked helm took his fancy we began to have serious doubts about our decision. Bosun could evade anyone on the dock; even a narrow jetty blocked by three of us was no barrier to his escalating shore-bound adventures. At last we all agreed he was not an ideal crew-member, and would need a career-change. As it happened, the New Zealand customs authorities were seeking intelligent determined dogs of his ilk to sniff out drugs, so off he went for his new apprenticeship. During later years, whenever our eldest son Ben cleared back into NZ entry ports as third mate aboard various P&O ships, he would brace himself for an embarrassingly enthusiastic welcome by his former canine crewmate during the random cabin contraband inspections.

Some furry critters find their way aboard without any encouragement. One of our most memorable stowaways was a half-grown bedraggled opossum which scrambled aboard one night while *New Zealand Maid* was in the final stages of preparation for the Chatham Islands yacht race. How far he had swum is anybody's guess, but he promptly took up residence in a safely inaccessible space under the aft fuel tank, where he slept by day and emerged tentatively once the crew were settled into their bunks next night, close enough to his bolt-hole to evade capture. After warnings from various fellow sailors that the Chatham Islands were opossum-free, our problem became more dire. With the race start scheduled for the next day, I waited up late, pillow at the ready. It was a merry chase once the little blighter had emerged and his escape route well stuffed. Opossums have sharp little claws and teeth, but he eventually acquiesced and allowed himself to be ferried ashore where he was last seen scrambling up the central pole of the marquee at the race HQ.

The last laugh was on us. On arrival we learned that the Chathams have been over-run with opossums for decades.

Rats are the age-old ship-board scourge. But they can make surprisingly friendly pets, as one of our sons revealed when he insisted on taking responsibility for a young white rat. By day Ratty lived in a cage at the end of the top starboard bunk, and in the evenings he would take his exercise by running up sleeves and out neck-holes of various boys (willing or not). It was not until we had a visit from a psychologist one evening that we discovered Ratty's dark side. Fixing a baleful glare at the unfortunate visitor, Ratty marched straight up and fixed his teeth firmly around his right index finger. Clearly white rats are programmed to fear and despise this particular breed of human.

The two-year life expectancy of rats was helpful in Ratty's case, as he conveniently expired not long before our next offshore voyage. However we once had one of his brown feral cousins take up residence aboard with less benign consequences. At first we were misled by his tiny droppings, assuming that he was merely a cute wee mouse. Weeks passed, and our ships provisions became progressively gnawed, along with various items of clothing and bedlinen. The droppings steadily became larger, and we could almost hear him laughing when he triggered the first mousetrap. One day we discovered he had chewed a tiny hole in our cardboard cask of red wine, and presumably had been lying on his back in the bag of rice directly beneath, enjoying a tipple.

When the depth sounder stopped working, our suspicions were confirmed that he was now cutting his teeth on *New Zealand Maid*'s wiring looms. This rat was going to have to either jump ship or have his two years on the planet compulsorily shortened. Our nightly regime now entailed emptying all lockers of anything edible, and resorting to traps of various types ranging from humane to dastardly. He laughed at them all, especially the occasion when I carried the tunnel trap for a mile down the road in my slippers one frosty night after being awakened as it snapped shut. As a parting gesture of goodwill I laid out a half apple as a gift before opening the trap and jumping clear. Imagine my chagrin to discover that he wasn't actually in it.

He appeared to enjoy the poison baits, carrying them off to his hidden lair for weeks. When he eventually ceased gnawing wires and baits, we were uncertain whether he had jumped ship or succumbed. There was certainly no smell of decaying rat in the bilges. It was over a year before the sad truth was revealed during a spring-clean – he had kept us guessing, even from the rodent underworld.

Some ocean voyagers are adamant that birds are the perfect shipboard pet. From our experiences with Ducky Tucker we weren't necessarily convinced, but certainly we've heard tales of parrots which have successfully coexisted for years aboard yachts significantly smaller than our own. However since the emergence of bird 'flu, quarantine officials have tended to take increasing notice of avian passengers, and we once met a European cruising couple who found themselves in expensive trouble when their Polly took it upon herself to do a little shore-bound exploration.

Of course not all shipboard passengers are of the furry or feathered kind. After discovering a pair of lizards taking up residence in the ratlines shortly after departing Bora Bora, we learned that it is expedient to dunk any bunch of bananas over the side for a good ten minutes before leaving port, as encouragement for any such potential stowaways to swim ashore.

At least reptiles aren't as unwelcome as various invertebrates which have often used their small size to stowaway aboard *New Zealand Maid* unannounced. Spiders are bad enough, but the annoyance of their cobwebs is partially compensated for by their ability to ensnare some of the less welcome small fly-in visitors. Mosquitoes are the typical bad-boys, especially in tropical zones plagued with malaria or dengue fever, however at least there are screening and repellent options for these annoyances. Weevils are a time-honoured ship-board nuisance too, their presence usually manifesting as tiny web-like evidence in our less perishable food supplies. Babs has a particular antipathy to cockroaches, and refuses to allow any cardboard boxes aboard that might be secretly housing these creepy-crawlies. Despite her vigilance we were once invaded by a bevy of large *flying* egg-laden cockroaches while anchored in Papeete, and even to this day the occasional cockroach trap turns up in the darkest corners of our lockers from time to time, as a legacy of the frenzy of activity which followed.

Human nature being what it is, even the most stringent red tape is unlikely to deter the opportunity for waifs in the league of *Goblin*'s Sinbad from being scooped up. The Nuku Hiva waterfront seemed to be over-run with dogs and roosters when we sailed in recently. The roosters gained their late afternoon exercise running from zealous youngsters who had been sent to catch a chook for dinner, while the dogs scrounged for fish offal as the local fleet returned. One particularly mangy dog had caught the attention of an Australian sailing couple with his mournful eyes. Crippled dogs like him stood little chance of competing against the boisterous pack, and he had learned during the past week that there were scraps and even whole hamburgers exclusively reserved for him at this table. Clearly this couple were smitten – despite the feeble wifi available on this island, they were hard at work investigating the options for the miserable creature. Would it be best to fly him ahead to Australia or sail him back? What quarantine obstacles would be awaiting his arrival? Where could dog provisions be purchased in this remote Marquesan archipelago.

Maybe we ocean wanderers are just a bunch of suckers. Anyone with an ounce of common sense would be taking a crateful of those roosters instead.

8

A Voyage to the Windiest Place in the World

(Adapted from *Snow Petrel* for *The Marine Quarterly*, Autumn 2016)

Fifteen hundred miles south of Tasmania, nestled into the Antarctic promontory of Cape Denison, is a tiny boat harbour less than two fathoms deep and half a cable wide. For roughly four weeks after each summer solstice, the annual fast-ice breaks out, leaving sufficient room for a single yacht, trussed on every quarter with shorelines stropped to boulders. It is a unique anchorage in a coastline dominated by thousands of miles of giant ice-cliffs.

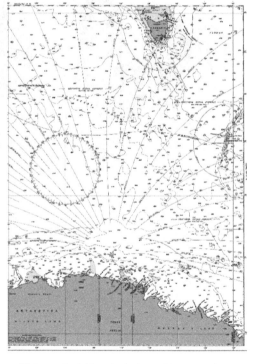

The *Antarctic Pilot* reveals some rather startling data on this extremely isolated location. For 284 days of the year the Cape is lashed with persistent winds of force 9 or greater. Mawson's Australian scientific team regularly recorded wind gusts over 200 mph during their incarceration here in 1912. What they hadn't known, when they established their small base here shortly after the summer solstice, was that behind their Baltic pine hut was a natural channel which funnelled the katabatic down-flow of freezing air from the inland icecap onto this stretch of coastline. It wasn't obvious when they arrived with a January high pressure system just offshore holding it at bay like a big dam. But when the Lows tracked past like giant vacuum cleaners, the pent-up sub-zero air mass would be sucked past their hut at unbelievable velocities.

No other location on the planet has recorded such an intense and prolonged wind-battering. The Pilot shows that the only months of significant reprieve from incessant katabatics are December and January, when summer anticyclones reduce the chance of being hammered to one day in two.

This was the little meteorological lottery which our son Ben planned to poke his nose into, 93 years later. He had recruited his youngest brother Matt as crew, and (on sufferance) allowed me to tag along as cabin-boy on my promise of good behaviour. Over the previous two decades about half a dozen well-funded large expedition yachts had attempted to reach Cape Denison – not all successfully. Ben's home-built steel Roberts 34 sloop *Snow Petrel* was only a fraction of their displacement, with a shoestring budget which could not even allow for a second-hand radar.

43°S Departure (Southern Tasmania, Jan 4, 2006):

I'm amazed how calm and happy Babs appears. She laughs and jokes with the rest of them, and to an onlooker she would seem to be waving us off for an afternoon fishing trip, not a voyage from which we might never return. We gather the lines and reverse out. Ben is determined to be under full sail as swiftly as possible. He has always hated engines, even as a small child.

He and I unshackle the anchor from its chain and bring it below to lash it among the foc'sle gear. We won't be needing it for a while now, and the weight is better low down and further aft. Not a moment too soon, with the bow beginning to gently lift and plunge as we meet the Southern Ocean swells. I glance at the GPS, already programmed to the waypoint of Cape Denison. It reads 1442 nautical miles nearly due south.

Roaring Forties, Day 2

Sched time. Our first radio contact since we've left land. Ben bought his HF marine set second hand for $100 not long before we left, mounting it deep inside his quarter-berth - the driest place in the boat, he had claimed. This evening I've decided to name it the 'radio cave', and despite our queasiness Matt and I are hovering around the companionway to listen to the comms.

For so many years I've been the one doing radio coms, and it's a humbling experience for me to be a mere cabin-boy listening to my son as skipper on that microphone. A yacht's radio voice is her mouthpiece. *Snow Petrel* tonight has become Ben himself to any ears out there.

Tonight, on four megs, Mike Harris, our live-aboard friend booms in. He's found some online GRIB files, predicting wind-speed and direction for up to a week ahead. The good news is that there's nothing sinister out there for us for a while, just two days of twenty to thirty knot westerlies.

He signs off. With barely a hesitation, Babs' voice fills the cabin. I'm stunned. When we left yesterday, *New Zealand Maid's* HF radio didn't seem to be working at all, and there was no time to fix it. She's spent all day stripping down all the vital wiring and remounting the aerial connections. Ben asks her to stand by and wriggles out of the cave so that I can slide in on my sensitive stomach for a quick chat.

Babs has overheard Ben hinting to Mike that his crew's a bit under the weather and she quizzes me in an embarrassingly loud voice. It's hard to keep secrets on the airwaves and you can't whisper, so I come clean and reassure her that it's a mere touch of queasiness, nothing too serious.

There are other ears out there too. My humiliation is complete. I slink off to my bunk for the remaining two hours of my watch off. Here the motion is cradle-like. Lying prone like this my stomach relaxes. On the deck directly above me I can hear the tramp of Ben's feet and the zip of his harness clip on the safety line as he does his rounds to the foredeck. It's a strange feeling to have reversed roles with my own son. At this instant I'm the weak one and he's demonstrating the invincibility that a child expects in a parent. I think back to his birth, to that tiny six-pound wrinkled specimen of humanity, helpless and so full of potential.

I hear him come below for Matt. There are the sounds of feet and winches, and I know they must be slabbing in a third reef. Then the rustle of wet weather gear being removed, and later the sound of Matt retching in his solitude....

KaBOOM! What a way to wake up. I feel *Snow Petrel* being pile-driven sideways for at least twenty metres. I stick my head up in the dome of the closed hatch to see Matt slouched safely in the shelter of the dodger. The beam seas are whitecapped and fairly steep but not high enough to be alarming. Getting the odd slammer like that is just the one in a hundred chance of being in the exact spot where a wave decides to break. It's like being inside a nine-ton steel bodyboard sideways-on to the surf.

It's nearly my watch anyway, so I get my gear on. We are now further south than I've ever sailed before.

Furious Fifties – Day 5

I've come off my midday watch and am decorating the whiteboard. 'WELCOME TO THE FURIOUS FIFTIES' reads the big one, footnoted '**PROCEED WITH CAUTION**'. A smaller one reads 'THE ROARING FORTIES FAREWELLS YOU – **THANK YOU FOR SAILING CAREFULLY.**' With three seconds of latitude to go I add a couple more: '**Beware strong winds**' and '**Whales crossing**'.

Three, two, one – WHOOPEE. *FIFTY SOUTH*! We celebrate with an early happy hour (a can of beer shared between the three of us, to Matt's disgust) with a plate of crackers and gherkins.

*Artist Roger Imms' impression of **Snow Petrel** alone in the Southern Ocean.*

Day 6   1415 hrs

The barometer is dropping like a stone – from 1010 to 991 since midnight. Ben managed to splice up a warp this morning for the drogue. Matt's been cooking up a huge casserole while it's not too rough, though *Snow Petrel* is already starting to corkscrew. Ben's most recent fax shows the Low centre almost right on top of us. We dumped the main completely on my midday watch and are now broad reaching under storm stays'l with only a scrap of genoa left unrolled. It's 45 knots out there already.

I'm resting in my sleeping bag for now, while Matt opens up the pressure cooker to check if it's ready. It's a huge pot of stew, enough for three days of bad weather – a lesson he's learned from his mum - and a delicious aroma fills the cabin. He calls Ben down to grab a feed while the going's good. Then, suddenly, our world comes unstuck.

I'm enveloped in a roar of noise, and gravity has strangely reversed. From my vantage point, pinned between the locker doors and the deck-head, I'm being squirted with water like a fire hydrant. I see Ben jammed in the open companionway door, one leg in and one still out. He is caught in a torrent of rushing water, his body stemming the flow of what otherwise would be an open sluice-gate. Matt is pinned against the galley cabin-side at the mercy of a still hot stove-top and a deluge of white water.

The sensation lasts long enough to register the sense of motion. We are moving sideways, very quickly. In fact *Snow Petrel* has become like a giant water-scoop, mast underwater, keel out, being driven sideways at twenty odd knots for fifty or sixty metres. Her deck is like the blade of a great bulldozer pushing water. Small wonder the supposedly watertight skylight is gushing all over me.

2130 hrs: We're pretty much cleaned up now and Matt managed to salvage enough stew from the back of the food lockers for a reasonable feed. The bilges are dry again and the electrics have survived. We're going to have to live with wet mattresses and sleeping bags for a while, but things could be a lot worse.

It's shrieking out there, between 50 and 60 knots maybe. The sea is a mass of foam with long streaks between each crest. We're doing watches mostly inside with our heads in the hatch dome, hanging on tight. But the motion has become lazier now that the drogue is out. It's a Seabrake plastic cone back there, a hundred metres behind us, weighed down with fathoms of chain. In flippant terms, I guess, that broach was nature's way of telling us to slow down and alter course. To broach is to be overpowered by a quartering sea so that the rudder can no longer keep a vessel on her course. In an instant she will slew around in a giant foaming skid until she is side-on to a breaking wave. The rest is up to the gods.

The fax tonight looked as if we're in the middle of a bullseye of isobar lines, so close together that they seem almost solid. But the barometer seems to have bottomed out. From now on things should steadily get better.

55° S, Day 7

Snow Petrel loved us when we hauled in the drogue this morning. She positively shook herself and kicked up her heels at the sense of freedom. She was labouring like a filly hauling a dray all night. But it was for her own good - and ours of course.

It's a special day today and even the sun is out to help us celebrate. There's a steady 17 knot nor'westerly and we're rollicking along under full sail. But it's markedly colder than yesterday. There are a lot more birds around, clouds of petrels and shearwaters, and some unusual cumulus on the horizon. Ben is convinced that we've crossed the convergence - that distinct transition line between cold Antarctic waters and the merely cool waters further north. To prove it he runs the thermometer under the galley seawater tap. It reads only five degrees compared with eight yesterday.

That gives us two reasons for a celebration, or three if you count the first fine day of the trip. We've decided to set the halfway point at 711 nautical miles to Cape Denison. That's half of the 1422 miles we had to go when we left Tasmania. We're expecting to get there at around 1400 hrs and Matt already has a chocolate cake in the oven. How he still manages to cook in bare feet I don't know. It's my watch so I'm popping up and down like a yoyo, accidentally standing on his bare toes while I'm licking the cake bowl. His slightly grumpy response is ludicrously self-controlled: 'I'd *appreciate* it if you wouldn't stand on my foot Dad'. (I'll swear we have the politest cook in the Southern Ocean.)

The cake comes out all heaped up in a corner of the cake dish like a sloping wave. The oven must have been unbalanced in its gimbals. The cake is a masterpiece though. It has become a landscape sloping down to the sea and iced in white. True to the chart of Cape Denison, it has a boat harbour of blue scalloped out of it, with a red jellybean boat securely anchored. On the shoreline is a convincing chocolate Mawson's Hut, and the whole landscape is littered with little black and white jellybean penguins. 'Cake Denison', he proclaims triumphantly, and we bargain over which parts of the landscape to eat first.

As this is a really special occasion, we share two beer cans between us to wash it down. The only thing to mar the occasion is the speed with which the barometer is dropping. Despite our banter, we are very aware that we are now out of reach of any effective rescue and we have to be self-sufficient.

Screaming Sixties – Day 11

I've re-decorated the whiteboard again. 'WELCOME TO THE SCREAMING SIXTIES – **EXTREME CAUTION NEEDED.**' Then – '**beware ice**', '**slippery when wet**', '**poor visibility**'. I'm leaving '**whales crossing**' on the board too.

It's a weird twilit night. There's simply no horizon and everything is a bland grey. The wind has nearly dropped and the sea's going glassy. The compass is still there in the hatchway, its little red light glowing, but now we're so close to the magnetic pole, the card is jammed on South.

I fire up the engine and try steering by the GPS but it's no good. Without any reference point, not even a star, the GPS track shows that I'm curving away to starboard, overcorrecting to port, and achieving little but a succession of letter S's. Maybe the fluxgate compass in the electric tiller pilot will still work? Ha! No show! We've just done a full figure-eight. Time to give up. I kill the engine, roll up the genoa and sheet the main in hard. Nothing to do but get my head-torch and read a book. Sooner or later we'll get some wind.

To liven things up I play a trick on Ben before I drag him out of his cold wet bunk for his watch. Sneaking down, I twist his left seaboot so that it faces backwards inside his wet weather gear. I try to suppress my laughter as I watch him sleepily trying to insert his toe into his heel space, hidden in the folds of his trousers. Finally he decides that he must be putting on the whole trouser-boot package back to front, so he reverses the lot and tries to climb in the wrong way round. Of course this time the other boot is wrong. Seeing me laughing, he cottons on to the joke and spends the next five minutes smugly setting up Matt's gear for an even more elaborate twist-up.

Icebergs - Day 13

We pass our first iceberg during Ben's watch, an interestingly sculpted castle with a turret at each end. Down to leeward is another, a tabular one probably a mile long, relatively boring in its rectangularity. Matt wants us to sail close to it, but Ben is spooked by its brash field, so we pose for some shots before Matt and I crawl back into our bunks. I'm reading *The Restaurant at the End of the Universe* and somehow it seems appropriate.

Pack Ice - Day 14

The horizon ahead is a low wall of white and gold. The sun hangs low in the southwest, emitting a golden light. To the north-east a nearly full moon glows in a pale blue sky. Ben is asleep and I delay calling him up until I'm sure the broken horizon is not a mere trick of light. Twenty minutes later there's no doubt left. We're motoring on a flat calm sea towards a seemingly impenetrable barrier, a jumble of white and golden shapes, angular and random.

Ben emerges from his bunk, suddenly awake and focused as he scans the approaching ice-edge with binoculars, searching for an opening to lead us in. Hearing our excited talk, Matt surfaces too, camera in hand - as always - and stifling a yawn. The photographer in him registers the colours, the sheer beauty of this setting. I marvel at how two young men from the same gene pool can focus on such different aspects when placed in an identical situation: Ben, the navigator/skipper, ever the practical one, and Matt, the artist - such unique and distinct individuals.

The visible horizon from *Snow Petrel's* cockpit, height of eye two metres, is only about three miles, and at five knots it doesn't take long to close the pack edge. There is barely time to break out some celebratory chocolate. Ben has donned gloves, hat and harness already and is preparing to run up the ratlines to scan ahead for leads. It's going to be a long and memorable night, even if it is one of perpetual light. We have reached 65° 43'S and are 77 miles from the ice cliffs of Antarctica.

As the sun's lower limb slowly angles to dip below the south-western horizon, we reach the pack. With no radiant warmth now, the air has a bite which numbs the lips and we find ourselves struggling to talk coherently. From aloft, Ben has identified a passage in. Standing with the tiller between my legs I steer us in.

We are motoring through what feels like a typical large river mouth, about a hundred metres wide and flanked by lumpy white stopbanks. We even have a few spectators waving - miniature tuxedo clad figures staring at us from their icy viewpoints and flapping in bewilderment.

From his perch far above me, Ben is scanning the distant expanse of white. Steering as I am with the tiller between my thighs, I can cradle my warm mug between both hands and absorb the heat. Aloft, Ben has no such luxury and has resorted to the little gel heat packs we purchased a lifetime ago in Hobart.

Ben is gesticulating excitedly, and I follow his gaze. A pair of white winged shapes is sweeping effortlessly astern of us, much more swiftly than the seabirds over the Southern Ocean rollers. Their agility is breathtaking, and briefly they slide across the face of the moon.

'Snow Petrels,' shouts Ben.

Meanwhile we're fast approaching a solid line of east-west ice. When Ben signals for me to turn to port I forget my lowly place as cabin-boy, and query his call. Mistake! Ben leaves no doubt who's captain of this ship. His air of authority, earned during years of responsibility on big ship bridge-decks, puts me firmly in my place.

Two twilit hours later we're still tracking eastward through an ice channel which stretches as far as the eye can see to the east. Embedded in the pack are several large icebergs which give the surreal terrain a false sense of permanence. Like isolated hills arising from a blue-white plain, they are useful steering references as we motor slowly along this wide lead. It is not a totally open channel, but the small isolated bergy bits scattered across our path are easy to avoid.

Ben is back in the cockpit now and I take the opportunity to climb the spreaders and survey the pack to our south. It is completely different from my earlier expectations. Rather than a solid mass of flat ice, it is a mixture of old and new sea ice, laid out in distinct bands. It is as if Antarctica, like Saturn, is surrounded by rings. The belt beside us is just one of several similar east-west belts cutting us off from our destination. To find an opening through the first wall would allow us only fifty or so metres to the next, and so on for as far as the limited southern horizon would reveal.

The southern sky is a radiant pink. Dusk and dawn have fused into a single transitional light-filled phase, and only Venus is visible, glowing in a pale blue sky.

Back on deck, I can see that Ben is worried. A light northerly has picked up and the whole field is beginning to move. At this stage, everything is moving in synch, and our channel is not squeezing up, but we wonder if our entry lead is closing behind us. It is a relief when Ben calls off our eastward search, and we begin to backtrack, noting how much our inbound GPS track has already been displaced sidewards.

Ben's face is a picture of exultation mixed with concern. The burden of responsibility is clearly sitting very heavily on his shoulders. He points out the differences between multi-year ice and sea ice, between heavy pack and three-tenths It has become clear to all three of us that he is the ice-master.

Someone needs to go below for an off-watch. Reluctantly I volunteer. This is the experience of a lifetime and I'm lapping it up, but we are going to have to discipline ourselves to sleep during the coming hours. The consequences of fatigue are too dire, and it is now that the value of having three rather than two to share helming duties is most apparent.

Four hours later, on watch alone in the cockpit with the engine barely above idle, I enjoy the unimaginable colours of the icescape around me. Some of the decaying bergy bits glow turquoise and emerald, and others are layered in browns and yellows. Two months ago the sea here was fast-ice with Emperor Penguins trudging over it. The flatter slabs now are the remnants of the winter's fast-ice, while the crazy angular stuff is probably multi-year slabs which have been fused together during successive winters. The larger chunks are likely to be fragments of ancient icebergs, calved off the cliff-like walls and sculpted by waves, wind and sun. The babies of the pack are the bits of brash, particles ranging in size from pots and pans to kitchen tables. We need to keep reminding ourselves that only ten percent of anything floating here is visible. The invisible ninety percent lurking beneath the surface will contain a mass equivalent to a sizable chunk of rock.

After two hours moving steadily southwards it becomes clear *Snow Petrel* is running out of clear water. It's not that this wide lead is narrowing but rather that it's becoming too choked with random chunks of loose pack for us to continue safely. In Ben's terms, I guess we are motoring into four-tenths pack. My real fear is the submerged shelves which lurk around the edges of the larger heavily decayed bergs.

I take her out of gear and wait for us to lose way. Ben, not surprisingly, shows up almost immediately, looking rather the worse for wear. He takes in the situation immediately and waits for me to run aloft. He doesn't seem surprised with my disappointing conclusion that there's no open sea in sight. There is no other option than to backtrack once more, this time to the north, and he disappears below again to grab a little more sleep while the going is safe.

Ahead is a labyrinth of leads through big multi-year pack ice.

1230 hrs: Over the past ten hours of feeling our way, we've made good only ten miles towards Antarctica but at least the ice has killed any seas. The pack has a different feel from last night. Gone are Saturn's rings. In their place is a confusing labyrinth of leads. We're under full sail now, and surprisingly I'm enjoying the challenge. At our mere three or four knots of boat speed, and without any sea running, the danger seems diminished. Ben is spending a lot of time aloft and has a strong hunch that there is open water not too far to the south. From his vantage point, he's cheating the maze and directs me left and right into ever-narrowing fresh leads while Matt is busy filming. I'm finding it a strain to continue under sail. Ben directs me into a tiny four-metre-wide gulch and I let go all sheets to reduce our way. As we ghost through the gap, I watch the pale green of a shallow shelf directly beneath our starboard side. My inability to control our speed is becoming a strain. Sails are doused and the intrusive noise of our engine spoils the solitude. No-one complains.

According to Ben's judgement we are now negotiating five-tenths ice surrounded with nine-tenths pack. Its saving grace is its layout and the fact that there is unmistakably open sea only two hundred metres to our south. The ice here is big multi-year stuff. At deck level we can't see over it. Ben's strategy is to zigzag our way through the tiny leads, and if necessary, nudge up to an obstacle and use the engine to shove it laboriously out of our way. Thankfully we don't need that option.

At five o'clock in the afternoon we make an abrupt exit from a high wall of ice into blue open sea. Antarctica is now a mere thirty miles away across open water. But where? At this distance, the coast should be visible. We scan the horizon. Below the distant line of light grey cloud is nothing but a horizon of blue sea.

Then the revelation hits me. I can't believe how easily our eyes have deceived us. Cloud line – phooee! We're looking at the grey-white skyline of the great continent itself and it's probably been visible all day.

Cape Denison - Day 15

This is a landfall like I've never experienced before. The cliff-tops, which I'm programmed to expect as green, are simply white - merging into a featureless smear of grey where the skyline meets the sky, devoid of any mountain range or even a single angle.

We heave-to behind a large iceberg for a while to get the big anchor on deck and inflate the tinker. Now as the GPS counts us down the last few miles, we're motoring easily in a moderate offshore breeze. The sun has been skulking behind the skyline for a couple of hours, but it's still daylight at 0100 hrs. We're just inside the Antarctic circle now and (drat) we missed a celebration. I'm chilled to the bone. There's a relentless bite to that breeze. Matt yells something and points. His eyes must be sharper than we thought. There on the grey-black promontory ahead is a *cross*, silhouetted starkly against the rose-tinted sky. We've read about the tragedy of Mawson's expedition, and the huge cross that he had erected to ease the pain of his comrades' deaths. And there it stands, over ninety years later, a poignant reminder of the historic interface between nature's impartiality and human endurance.

With the chart on hand we motor under Cape Denison, turn right at the one-third point across the entrance to Boat Harbour, and creep slowly into the inlet towards Mawson's Hut. The sounder rises to less than three metres, then levels off.

Even above the clatter of *Snow Petrel's* diesel we can hear an awful din, an unfamiliar staccato braying. But we are too preoccupied to fully register the sheer numbers of Adele penguins clustered among the grey and white landscape.

I'm on the foredeck struggling with the lashings on the giant fisherman anchor. My gloved fingers refuse to work. The delicate operation of untying even a simple slipknot is beyond my power. In desperation I resort to a knife. *Snow Petrel's* bow is beginning to sheer away towards the eastern rocks as the chain rattles out. Twenty, thirty, forty metres. I throw a couple of turns on the bollard to let her pull up, then turn to Ben for his intentions. Too much chain and we could sheer from side to side, crunching rocks in the process. 'Let go the lot!' His command is so decisive I don't even query it. Sixty metres is a lot of chain. We'll need every metre of it in here when the next hundred knot katabatic hits us.

The tinker looks like a toffee apple when we launch it, glazed in a smooth layer of ice, and the outboard takes ages to start, despite Ben's precaution of checking that it was working earlier in the day.

Ben and Matt both want to set foot on land straight away which is fine by me. It's like a freezer out there and I'm happy to wait till later when the sun's well up. So my function is to keep the kettle and thermos full of hot water, and to feed them rope out of this giant coil as they search the shore for suitable fastening points. The advantage of being in charge of hot water is that I get to mind the hot-water bottles while the boys are playing around ashore. I've found some good spots to mind them too. Two stuffed inside my jacket and another wrapped in a towel where I can put my hands in very regularly to check it's still warm.

Four hours later, we are secure, all sitting on the settees. Hot chocolate for everyone and a hot-water bottle each while we talk - buzzing, a babble of talk. We've actually done it! Made it to Antarctica! Somehow it doesn't seem real. I break out the rum. There are no watches to keep now. And we talk… talk… talk. It all pours out, two months' worth of hopes and fears. So much that could have gone wrong. Storms, dismasting, ice-collisions, engine or transmission failure, injury…. Yet here we are, our little team, unscathed so far, and in good spirits.

The rum loosens our tongues, and the banter begins. I pour a second glass all round then squirrel the bottle away for another occasion. We are a team, a bunch of good mates.

Then sleep, glorious, glorious sleep.

***

Snow Petrel at Cape Denison with five shorelines and 60m chain.

9

Trouble in Antarctica – the *Shokalskiy* Debacle

(This misadventure, eight years later, puts the success of our Snow Petrel voyage into a whole new perspective).

There is something very wrong aboard our ship this evening. The sensation is distinctly different from the rhythmic lift-halt-crunch of an icebreaker on a regular day. It is impossible to ignore the shuddering vibration of both labouring engines, or the unpredictable jolting motion. In the compact passenger lounge, nervous laughter and uneasy glances accompany each violent sideways lurch, and voices are raised to be heard over the screech of tortured steel. Not everyone knows it, but tonight *Akademik Shokalskiy* is fighting for her life.

At 0400 hrs, Akademik Shokalskiy came to a shuddering halt!

Sleep in our tiny cabins is virtually impossible. Occasionally an ice tower slides slowly past the port-hole, visible through blizzard-driven snow in the perpetual daylight. So when all motion abruptly ceases at 0400hrs, the silence is as threatening as the struggle that preceded it.

We are in Eastern Antarctica. It is Christmas Eve 2013. We are a long way from any possible support, and the immediate future of the 74 people on board has just unravelled.

Akademik Shokalskiy began her life as a USSR spy-ship plying high-latitude waters during the last phase of the cold war. Although not a true icebreaker – her V-shaped bow section differs markedly from the spoon shape of an ice-crushing vessel - she was registered as a class 1A ice-strengthened vessel of a modest 71.6 metres and 1753 tonnes displacement. In more recent years, although still Russian-owned, she had been converted to carry up to 50 passengers. For the voyage I am describing, she was under charter to a scientific party from Sydney's University of NSW. In addition to her 22 Russian crew members, she carried 6 staff and 46 passengers, half of whom were tourists. The remainder included 3 journalists, a small heritage team (including Babs and me) and a group of science academics.

The rationale behind this odd mix of passengers was simple enough. The cost of the expedition was some two million dollars, and the sponsorship offered by Google and a major Australian bank had left a half-million-dollar shortfall, which was made up by offering a group of science-minded tourists the chance to participate in polar oceanographic observation work. There was also the hint of a possible visit to one of the world's least accessible polar heritage sites – Mawson's Huts at Cape Denison, 800 km west of the Ross Sea.

I had first visited this patch of water and its coastline of ice-cliffs eight years earlier, aboard *Snow Petrel*. Only a handful of large expedition yachts have ever attempted this feat. *Snow Petrel* was the most recent, and by far the smallest. (Two decades later, none have succeeded since.)

Out of that voyage arose a personal interest in the preservation of the huts built by Sir Douglas Mawson's scientific expedition in 1912. I returned for six weeks in 2007 aboard the French icebreaker *L'Astrolabe* as deputy leader of a heritage team, and more recently had led a team constructing an exact replica of the historic hut on Hobart's waterfront. The Mawson's Huts Foundation seized upon the *Shokalskiy* expedition as a chance to send our small team back to Cape Denison for urgent assessment and maintenance work. This would not, however, be a straightforward trip. Global warning had complicated our access options since an environmental catastrophe in 2010.

This part of the world now experiences an increasing concentration of sea-ice. The reasons are complex, but all are a result of climate change. Basically, as ice thaws, it produces fresh water, which floats over the denser salt water, and freezes at a higher temperature. The local environment at Commonwealth Bay has also been massively affected by an event 1500 km to the east, where a 140 km-long iceberg broke away from the Ross Sea Ice Shelf in 2008. This megaberg spent two years drifting slowly westward in the polar counter-current, bulldozing off the 60 km long tongue from the Mertz glacier just east of Commonwealth Bay before breaking in half. The residual iceberg, a 70 km-long beast named B09B, then ran aground directly to the north of Cape Denison.

The year-round fast ice which immediately formed around it has since spelt disaster for the local breeding colonies of Adele penguins. It also prevented any Mawson's Huts Foundation maintenance expeditions after 2010. By 2013 the summer ice-edge was 70 km NW of Cape Denison, too far for *L'Astrolabe*'s helicopter to shuttle expeditioners and cage-pallets. The *Shokalskiy* had no helicopter, but she carried two quadbikes and three Argo vehicles - comical-looking things resembling eight-wheeled beach-buggies. The best one had tracked wheels, a windscreen, and a Briggs & Stratton engine. The older two were untracked and decidedly worse for wear. The proposal was for our three-strong team and a handful of science academics to make the hitherto untried journey across the sea ice to the huts in two of these vehicles.

*

Unloading the Argos at the ice-edge of the (safest) western polynya

Our departure from NZ's southern-most port of Bluff in early December was an exciting experience. Babs and I have covered some 90,000 miles at sea, but almost all of these have been under sail. *Akademik Shokalskiy* was definitely no luxury cruise ship, but there was something honest about this functional, unstabilised vessel, whose motion reminded us of our own ketch. The Russian crew were clearly confident and experienced Like most of the passengers, we were full of anticipation for what the coming four weeks would bring. *Akademik Shokalskiy* carved her way south through pack ice into an ice-free polynya beside the western flank of B09B, reaching the fast-ice edge about 70 km from Mawson's Huts, as expected. Various scientific activities continued as we spent three days searching out an over-ice route for the drive to Cape Denison. It was a tough trip, navigating around tide-cracks and impassable ridges. Wherever an iceberg was embedded in the ice-plain, its 'bow-wave' of pressure ridges made progress impossible. Whenever the untracked Argo became bogged in snowdrifts, the tracked one would be needed for a tow.

Happily the greatest threat – Cape Denison's notorious 100-knot katabatic winds – held off during the two days allocated for our maintenance work at the century-old huts. It was a relief to navigate our way back via GPS waypoints, arriving at the ship five days before Christmas.

My Argo in a tide crack

At this point, the university expedition leaders made a fateful decision. The ship would spend two days forging her way clockwise around B09B to a point near its *eastern* flank. As sailors, this decision left Babs and me distinctly uneasy. All significant winds in this region are from the eastern quarter, and the circumpolar current sweeps constantly in from the east, flowing under any fast ice in its path. This change of location would effectively place the ship on a potential lee ice-shore. The reasons they gave for this fateful decision were twofold. Firstly, there was potential scientific observation work to be done in the vicinity of the marginally accessible Hodgeman Islets. Secondly, it would give the paying passengers an opportunity to set foot on Antarctic rock.

We arrived at the eastern ice-edge in the early hours of 23rd December. To our northeast was relatively open water sprinkled with light pack. Upwind, three medium-sized bergs were embedded in the fast-ice sheet. A few kilometres further east was the former location of the Mertz

Glacier's 60 km long ice-tongue, which satellite ice-charts still displayed as a blank outline despite its disappearance, masking any pack-ice in the vicinity. The weather forecast predicted 25 knot SE winds rising to a 40 knot ESE blizzard later in the day and 50 knots SSE next day. It was already too windy for the ship to lie beam-on to the ice-edge, so the captain's only option was to hold the bow into a notch in the ice, with one engine idling in gear during the day. This enabled the quadbikes to be craned onto the ice from the foredeck hold. The passengers would be ferried by zodiac, and the Argos were to be floated ashore.

These little vehicles are designed to be amphibious, and have a plastic tub-like body. The untracked wheels are capable of self-propulsion at 2 knots in calm flat water. In water, though, the tracked version has no effective propulsion, and has to be towed. The wheeled versions made it to the ice edge, but the tracked Argo was towed too fast and filled with water, kept afloat only by the air in its tyres and clearly now unusable.

By this time it was lunchtime and visibility was diminishing due to blowing snow. However during lunch, the astonishing decision was announced by the university expedition leaders that the two surviving Argos and two quad bikes would take passengers over the fast-ice to the Hodgeman Islets 9 km to the SSW. The Russians were clearly not impressed.

The first group of academics and paying passengers left at around 1300hrs. Snowdrifts slowed their progress, and each round trip took over 45 minutes. Our heritage team declined to participate - the view from the ship's bridge was sufficiently interesting for us. Igor, our experienced captain, was clearly agitated, and was fixated on the radar screen. At around 1430 he made an abrupt VHF request for an immediate recall of all shore parties. Huge quantities of pack ice were closing in rapidly from the southeast.

Pack ice in this part of the world comprises hundreds of thousands of large chunks of ice, ranging in size from kitchen tables to double-decker buses. It is constantly on the move, carried by ocean currents and surface wind. The hazard it poses is similar to the crush of a river full of logs during flood. Unlike logs, though, pack ice has the ability to bond together under pressure.

Captain Igor must have been very conscious of the rapidly encroaching danger. Although we could hear the hand-held VHF calls from the zodiac crew trying to relay his request to the drivers, there was no response. On the bridge we waited tensely for the Argos to return. Half an hour later an Argo emerged from the drifting snow, discharged four passengers - and then, to our astonishment, loaded six more and disappeared through the blowing snow back towards the islets.

It appears that the hand-held VHF radios were either switched off or out of range. It was over three hours after the urgent recall before the last group of passengers arrived back at the ice-edge, and a further half hour before the vehicles were loaded aboard. Our view from the bridge through the blowing snow was of a crush of pack ice as far as the eye could see.

For the next ten hours, the ship laboured through dense pack ice under great pressure, covering less than 2 km. The ice continued to pile up to our east. By the time Igor shut down the engines there was 5km of log-jammed pack ice between the ship and open water. As we had our breakfast the ship was strangely silent, despite the shriek of a 50-knot SE blizzard across the icy decks. It was Christmas Eve.

Akademik Shokalskiy, critically beset

We were assembled for a reassuring briefing: "Soon the wind would change, and the ice would all blow away." These reassurances were less than convincing! In the polar low-pressure belt, easterlies are as much a fact of life as in the trade-wind belt. The ship was developing a list to port. Meanwhile the sound of sledgehammers near the bows had us all puzzled, until one adventurous spirit braved the snowdrifts on the foredeck and came back reporting a two-metre-long hole near the port bow. An ice tower had ripped the hull open just above the strengthened section, and the Russian crew were doing some hardcore panel-beating.

Christmas morning had us mustered for another briefing by the university expedition leaders. First the good news: there would be a Christmas celebration in the bar later. Then the bad news: two icebergs were ploughing through the pack towards the ship. One was likely to pass closer than 300 metres from our bow. The captain had activated a distress call via GMDSS to the International Maritime Rescue Coordination Centre at Falmouth, UK. Three icebreakers had been directed to come to our immediate assistance.

Immediate assistance in Antarctica is measured in days rather than hours. The closest vessel – France's *L'Astrolabe* - was halfway to Hobart from Dumont D'Urville Base. The powerful Chinese icebreaker *Xue Long* was also about two days away, steaming towards the Ross Sea from the west. And Australia's *Aurora Australis* had just arrived at Casey Station, about 2500 km to the west.

For the next two days the easterly blizzard continued to rage, gusting to 60 knots. The pressure on the hull from millions of tonnes of pack ice to windward was clearly evident to leeward, where the hull had been acting like a giant bulldozer blade, pushing up a mass of jumbled ice. The list to port steadily increased to 4° - not a lot for those of us used to a heeling yacht, but enough to make life uncomfortable. There were now 40 km of compressed pack ice between us and open water. On the plus side, the icebergs were no longer a threat, and the damaged bow now had a door-sized patch welded over the hole.

Our view of Xue Long through a telephoto lens

L'Astrolabe and *Xue Long* arrived in the polynya of relatively open water 50km to our east on 27th December. The French icebreaker had no helicopter, and had developed engine trouble. She stood by in the safety of light pack while the Chinese ploughed on in. Our briefings had emphasised the ability of this powerful icebreaker to break us out. She was over twice *Shokalskiy*'s length and twelve times her displacement, and her 20,000hp was seven times more power than that of our two engines combined. There was much excitement when someone spotted her, a red blob in the distant whiteness. She came to within 10km of us before coming to a halt. And there she stayed, on a constant bearing, the next day, and the next.

There were assurances that *Xue Long* was 'maintaining a holding pattern', but it did not take long to work out that she too, with her 110 Chinese scientists and crew, was now beset. The French ship was given clearance from the Australian MRCC to stand down, and started limping north for Hobart on her crippled engine. Meanwhile, the Chinese ship's captain steadfastly refused to make any formal request for assistance.

Three days passed, with the weather slowly easing and the ice pressure reducing. Ballast tanks were juggled to reduce our list. *Xue Long*'s big KA37 helicopter made a single overpass one afternoon before visibility closed in once more. The mood aboard *Akademik Shokalskiy* was generally upbeat. The immediate danger appeared to have passed. The Australian *Aurora Australis* was on her way, although we were unpleasantly aware that she was significantly smaller and only half as powerful as *Xue Long*, and as she had no helicopter aboard there was no clear picture of how events would unfold when she arrived.

It would be easy to assume that we had an option of using the Argos to begin transferring personnel. But the compacted pack-ice in which our ships were beset was of a totally different composition from annual fast-ice (where a relatively smooth metre-thick plain was broken only by occasional pressure-ridges and tide-cracks). Surrounding us now was a disjointed jumble of jagged shapes, fused together and layered with a snow blanket. No vehicle could hope to travel across this surface, and travel on foot would be hazardous due to a multitude of deadly voids lurking beneath the surface.

Aurora's arrival in the open polynya to our east brought little comfort. Her skipper made two attempts to enter the ice-field, pulling back after less than 3km each time. Experts were decreeing that the ice surrounding us was likely to remain as a permanent field for a year or longer. *Akademik Shokalskiy* and possibly *Xue Long* could suffer the same fate as Shackleton's *Endurance*, incidentally causing the worst environmental disaster in East Antarctica's history.

A week passed. New Year's Eve arrived. Negotiations in difficult English aimed at attempting a helicopter evacuation were afoot between all three captains. Igor, running short on fuel and food, was adamant that all his passengers must go, as well as the Russian female crew members. This produced a near-mutiny, as these half-dozen women were in relationships with male crew members, and eventually he relented. His intention was to remain with the ship for up to six weeks in the hope of a break-out.

By now politics had entered the fray. Negotiations were underway to order the US *Polar Star*, at 90,000 hp the world's most powerful icebreaker, to our vicinity. That evening Igor fielded not one but two satellite calls from the Russian foreign minister demanding that he avoid the national disgrace of being rescued by Americans, and the Chinese were equally horrified.

Meanwhile there was a general consensus that an evacuation of everyone aboard *Akademik Shokalskiy* (except those retained by the vessel's master) should take place as soon as practicable. The difficulty was how to implement it. *Xue Long* had a helicopter capable of ferrying passengers, but it had too large a blade diameter to land on *Aurora Australis'* flight deck. Meanwhile the Australian captain was not prepared to allow passengers to step on to the ice, as he was unhappy about the hazards involved. The standoff continued through New Year's Eve, the celebrations muted by the stipulation that alcohol consumption should be limited so we would be in a fit state to be safely disembarked at short notice if the situation changed. It was a rather memorable evening nonetheless.

Our first day of 2014 brought a strong sense of déjà vu. Since the Chinese helicopter's short flight four days earlier, strong winds and poor visibility had kept it firmly grounded on *Xue Long*'s flight deck, and today was no better. There was no comfort in the fact that the embarrassing truth about the Chinese ship's besetment had been broken to the world media. The most significant event for us was the very slow movement of an orange speck across our horizon. *Aurora Australis* had succeeded in crunching a kilometre closer to the huge Chinese ship, and halted next to a level floe stable enough to be used as a helipad.

When the evacuation was ordered late next day, things happened very fast. A crude landing zone was marked out with soy sauce and powdered drinking chocolate on a relatively flat embedded floe near *Shokalskiy*, and the Chinese flew in. A dozen orange-clad figures leapt from the huge hovering chopper, laying down wide planks to spread the load of the runners. We formed a human chain to transfer dozens of freeze-dried food containers which had been sent from the Australian ship to help sustain the Russian crew. It was an emotional time, seeming very wrong to be whisked away in groups of ten, leaving so many Russians and Chinese to an uncertain future; though by now we knew that (despite national pride), the huge US *Polar Star* had been despatched to render further assistance.

There is an irony in the final turn of events. Our 52 evacuees spent a further month aboard the Australian icebreaker, diverting back to Casey Station before discharge in Hobart. Meanwhile, Polar Star had not yet reached the stricken vessels when against all odds the entire 30-km wide icefield began to pivot anticlockwise as a solid mass. Both ships were lucky enough to work their way out before the next SE gale slammed the fracture-line leads shut again. The Russian crew were back in civilisation before we were.

The Chinese KA37 lands on our crudely marked adjacent floe

*

The wheels of bureaucracy turn slowly. Nearly two years later, litigation was still proceeding. Accusations of negligence and incompetence were flying, though thankfully the ship's officers and crew were not implicated. Seven-digit compensation claims were being made, accompanied by much ill feeling - some of it perhaps justified. But things could have been distinctly worse. Red faces pass. Body-bags are for keeps.

***

10

Deliveries

For those of us who spend time wandering oceans, there is some comfort in the old adage:

"God does not deduct from a man's allotted span, his time spent sailing".

After due consideration, however, I am convinced that this adage does *not* include yacht deliveries. Indeed, the opposite may well be true.

Delivery may seem an innocent enough word, but mention it to a boxer, drug dealer, midwife, postman or sailor, and you may well notice a shadow flicker across his or her face. A memory, perhaps, of some past occasion when well-formulated plans became unstuck. As a conversation starter in most sailing circles, it is a word guaranteed to catalyse an evening's-worth of entertainment and knowledge-sharing (second only to the subject of marine toilets).

There was a time, in my more innocent years, when the offer of a paid yacht-delivery would lift my spirits. Being paid cash to go sailing seemed too good to be true, especially during those heady days when any available income was being consumed by the half-finished hull of our 45ft ketch, and the mouths of a rapidly expanding brood of sons.

As I ease into my wiser years, a small cautioning bell rings inside my head with any proposal for a vessel relocation. Strangely enough, these offers are invariably couched with glowing reports of seaworthiness, along with multiple reasons for why the owner is sadly unable to deliver the vessel himself.

The waters surrounding New Zealand and Australia can, on occasions, provide for pleasant sailing. However, distances between safe havens are often considerable, and Tasman Sea weather systems can cycle rapidly. Coastal currents, sudden fronts and wind-slots are thrown in as well, to keep life interesting. Babs and I have sailed these waters often enough in our own gaff ketch to be conscious of the quirks of various stretches of coastline. Throw in an unfamiliar vessel with a deadline, and the variables increase exponentially.

One of our good mates, a highly competent yachtsman whom we shall re-name as Laurie for the purpose of anonymity, has survived three total losses since he began his delivery career in these waters, not to mention more trivial misadventures such as dismasting and engine-room inferno. In his defence, these incidents relate to a very small percentage of his substantial sea-mileage. In fairness too, it is also worth mentioning that one sinking was due to whale collision, and another resulted from being towed at excessive speed with a gaping hole where the rudder should have been.

Despite the occasional rather unfortunate outcome, Laurie's overall delivery track record illustrates a considerable degree of optimistic enthusiasm, for he has also gained fame for some spectacularly successful deliveries. One entailed salvaging a burnt-out insurance write-off – a 45-ft production yacht located at a remote Cook Island atoll during the Pacific hurricane season. The alloy mast had been shortened because of the extreme heat, concertina fashion, near the partners. All glass ports had exploded, and sails were seriously compromised. The standing rigging needed length adjustments, with the simple deployment of multiple bulldog grips. More inconveniently, a considerable number of items of essential hardware had mysteriously disappeared, and were only able to reappear once certain local palms had been crossed with silver, so to speak. One particularly curious permanent disappearance was the fuel lift-pump diaphragm. (The engine had miraculously survived the heat, along with all joinery below knee level.) The mind boggles at what possible value such an innocuous component would have had for the local islanders. In desperation Laurie procured a bicycle inner tube which he proceeded to cut into diaphragm-sized pieces. The five-hour life expectancy of each disk of rubber, once deployed, added to the legendary status of this particular delivery voyage, and nearly spelled disaster at the eleventh hour when the second-last diaphragm failed within a cable's length of Wellington Harbour's Barrett's Reef in a 50 knot nor'wester.

Our nineteen-year-old son Dan was a party to another one of Laurie's more spectacular successful deliveries. Babs and I had been approached to deliver a Greenpeace yacht to New Zealand from Moruroa Atoll, shortly after all of the impounded protest vessels were released by the French Military. This particular run-down former liveaboard sloop, *La Ribaud* had been purchased for a peppercorn price for the sole purpose of conveying a bunch of Pacific Island politicians and journalists into the prohibited zone at the nuclear test site. Its sadly neglected engine had failed on the first day out of port, and after a gruelling two-week upwind passage from Tahiti their arrival and immediate arrest inside the prohibited zone was apparently a blessed relief.

La Ribaud was *not* a good example of an ideal delivery yacht, especially for the 3000-mile impending voyage to New Zealand. She had no engine, no electrical charging capability (hence no nav lights or HF radio) and no liferaft. Babs and I politely declined the request, as we were (fortuitously) committed to run the fishing ketch *Sunniva* during the Tuna season (and had not long returned from three months aboard our own ketch at the test zone). But the chance for a little excitement was too much for both Laurie and our son Dan. From the moment they were towed out of the test zone until the day that they were towed into Auckland Harbour a month later, there was little news of their progress or fate. On arrival, Dan did admit privately that he would never go voyaging again on such a sparsely equipped yacht.

Over the years Dan and various of our other four sons have crewed on a number of our own interesting deliveries. I consider myself to be a reasonably well-prepared skipper, and Babs is the epitome of caution. However despite this we have had our own share of delivery incidents, most of which tended to occur after agreeing to relocate a 'well-equipped vessel' sight unseen.

One such occasion involved collecting a 40ft sloop from New Zealand's remote southwestern coast of Fiordland, and delivering to Nelson via the exposed west coast in mid-winter. On paper the yacht sounded great. The inventory was pored over diligently, with the owner agreeing to finance certain extra items that we insisted be added. Our very considerable fee was accepted without a murmur, along with a chartered helicopter to fly us in through the blizzard conditions. *Wild South* had been deployed as a remote houseboat for a crayfishing couple for the previous five years. On arrival we discovered that she had been furnished with every conceivable 240-volt appliance, all running through an inverter which was crudely crocodile-clipped to the house-batteries, directly below the cockpit drains. When we realised that all lighting was also running through same inverter, our internal alarm bells began ringing, by which time the helicopter had disappeared through the driving snow.

It was one of those deliveries that we prefer to put out of our minds. The fifty-knot easterly was thankfully an offshore wind on this normally lee shore, but the persistent blizzard made helming rather chilly, especially as the autopilot would only helm us anticlockwise. When thirteen-year-old Josh reported water over the cabin-sole in the middle of the first night, Babs had the sense to taste it and declare it relatively fresh. Closer examination (after unscrewing a bulkhead hatch) showed fanbelts in direct contact with various items of plumbing. This same inspection revealed that the bilge pump emptied directly into cockpit drains which had worked loose and were busy recycling fresh and salt water back into bilges via the battery box.

The owners seemed relieved and somewhat surprised when we berthed in Nelson three days later. They shrugged off our apologies for the soggy shag-pile carpet and non-functioning kitchen appliances. Our rather lengthy list of recommended maintenance work was pocketed with barely a glance. The trip had topped up our piggybank as well as our bank of accrued nautical wisdom.

This accrued knowledge comes in very handy at times too. On one memorable occasion, delivering a 34-footer for 200 miles across Bass Strait in light conditions, a barely discernable rise in engine pitch at change of watch, followed by a distinct loss of speed, jogged my memory of a desperate experience on the protest flotilla sloop *Joie*. Bolting downstairs, I was just in time to discover oily bilgewater lapping the cabin sole. Dan was my accomplice at the time, and I was thankful for his slender stature. While I laboured with the underfloor bilge pump, kneeling in a film of diesel, Dan squeezed into a tiny space well aft to plug the hole which *should* have been housing our curiously *absent* propeller shaft. At some stage during the thirty-odd years since this Duncanson had been launched, an ambitious owner had rather rashly installed an additional fuel tank snugly above the stuffing box, and then re-powered with a larger engine, retaining the original slim shaft. Sailing into the Port Philip rip at the heads next day was a test of our skills, and the rather startled owner attempted to persuade me to sign an insurance statement that his missing propeller was the result of entanglement in a craypot line. This I would not do. Admittedly in our pre-inspection we had failed to notice that the well-concealed shaft was badly scored from long term contact with an exhaust wet-lock, but I was certainly not going to compromise my reputation by insinuating that we didn't maintain a sharp lookout under way.

It is often the small details that are the most significant. During a brief engine inspection while pausing at Gisborne midway through a 600-mile delivery passage from Wellington to Auckland aboard a 36ft steel ketch, Ben's curiosity was aroused by a needle-thin black string dangling from the oil-pressure sensor into a disturbingly black sump. It was only during inspection, when I attempted to grasp it and discovered that the supposed string was actually black *fluid*, that I realised that we were about to dodge a bullet. I prefer not to tarnish my reputation by arriving with a seized engine, which would likely have resulted from an oil leak of this significance. We were already somewhat twitchy on this delivery, as the previous owner had drawn our attention to the exceptionally rusty plating in the vicinity of the rudder stock. Heightened watchkeeping duties included an hourly inspection of the affected area, but on arrival all was still well. It wasn't until we received a message from the new owner, a week later, that he had accidentally holed his proud new ketch with a screwdriver through the rusty plating *under the galley stove* that we realised how lucky we had been.

Several of our deliveries have been on vessels which have been laid up awaiting a sale. Electrical corrosion issues seldom show up until systems have been livened up for a day or three. One notable example occurred on a 54ft ketch shortly after departing Fremantle for delivery to Sydney via the Australian Bight. *Kela* was a vessel we knew well enough, having sailed in company with her on a midwinter Roaring Forties passage a few years earlier. However she had been languishing in a broker's berth for two years, and we were barely a day out on this two-week passage when the first item failed; the fluxgate compass and with it the entire autopilot that we had so much been looking forward to enjoying. Two days later the GPS coax cable failed, and it took some fancy repairs with aluminium foil to jury-rig the aerial. Next day was the turn for the HF radio to die. After that, one by one, various items of sail wardrobe began to fail, largely at the seams. We literally stitched our way across across the Bight, and were certainly glad to have two teenage sons aboard to share the work. As for the delivery fee – it kept us cruising for the next six months.   *Kela*

The common thread that we share with our mate Laurie is our approach to crisis management – a nice cup of the good old British elixir of life. We both firmly believe in the indispensability of a mug of tea for clearing the head and settling the nerves. Indeed Laurie maintains that this policy has saved his life on at least one occasion, after being driven ashore on NZ's remote Ninety Mile Beach, single-handing a 55ft steel ketch southwards during a nor'west gale. It was the cup of tea that he forced himself to brew while huge breakers slammed into his dying vessel that did the trick. Quelling that instinct to hurl himself into the violent waters and swim ashore, his life-saving brew allowed sufficient time to pass for the tide to fall sufficiently for him to step onto damp sand.

As I write, comfortably snugged down on a four-ton mooring block in New Zealand's far north, *New Zealand Maid* is surrounded by mid-voyage round-the-world cruising yachts, their owners waiting out the hurricane season and reviewing their plans. A few husband-wife couples are faltering in their resolve.

"Do you know anyone who might be able to sail our yacht back to Frisco? She's a great boat, really well set up." *I cock an eyebrow at Babs. Her face remains passively non-committal.*

"If we hear of anyone we'll let you know."

***

11

"Do you ever get scared?"

"Do you get scared when it's rough?" It is a school-visit question which outnumbers any other, three to one, and is one that I rather dread, as it defies a simple answer and inevitably leads to a less than satisfactory response.

A child's concept of 'being scared' does not necessarily correlate with the all-consuming stomach-knotting head-spinning ear-roaring vision-blurring fear that renders one's judgement impotent during a truly terrifying experience.

I remember being scared as a child, in the bow of a smallish centre-boarder as it rose and fell on grey-green waves, in the knowledge of great depths extending far below – far deeper than my small body could ever survive. It was a brief fear, soon overcome by a realisation that buoyancy would overcome each approaching wave, and that I could trust this vessel to carry me safely back to harbour.

This 'epiphany of buoyancy' has carried me confidently into a voyaging adulthood that has introduced the wider concept of perils at sea. There have certainly been occasions, running before a Roaring Forties gale under bare poles and drogue, when spume-laden greybeards astern have hinted at overwhelming our vessel. These are times when a firmly closed companionway hatch and a thermos of tea allow skipper and crew to think rationally on Archimedes' laws of displacement.

These are also times when it helps to have confidence in the vessel's structural resilience. We began building our own ketch in the backyard when we were poverty-stricken students, however there were no compromises in strength during the build. Whenever white water sweeps *New Zealand Maid*'s decks and cabin, it helps to know that I had the foresight to add a good many more fastenings than specified, back during those heady days when we were scratching to feed our kids.

Looking aft in such heavy weather, with seas sometimes appearing higher than our mizzen mast, the swirl of our disturbed wake on the face of each following wave tends to have a curious effect. To port and starboard, we see white water cascading past barely metres away, yet we are rising and falling on unbroken water. Of course, this is not always the case. Converging gale-driven wave trains call for steadier nerves. During a Southern Ocean knockdown aboard *Snow Petrel* en route to East Antarctica, my first reaction was more a sense of bewilderment than one of fear, as icy water sluiced through the cabin while gravity reversed. Perhaps if the outcome had been more life-threatening our personal reactions may have been different, but there was no stomach-knotting or head-spinning during the immediate aftermath, just an urge to clean up and set a drogue.

Our eldest son Ben recounts a more serious incident aboard a 28ft double-ender that pitchpoled en route to Tonga. He saw the pair of enormous vertical-faced waves almost upon him from his lonely position in the cockpit just before the sensation of being engulfed in green water and subsequently surfacing - tethered - near the wallowing hull. Rather than fear, he speaks of a sense of déjà vu, a recollection of a similar incident as a child being jettisoned from his tiny P-class sailing dinghy by a breaking wave outside Napier harbour. Then the sense of self-preservation kicked in, along with the steps necessary to get back aboard and begin setting things right.

In such circumstances fear is truly the enemy. Various acquaintances have made decisions to abandon their yacht after capsizing, initiating difficult rescue operations only to later learn that their supposedly sinking vessel had been discovered very much afloat near some distant archipelago.

Perhaps I have been lucky, and Neptune still has a set of truly terrifying waves with my name on them. But to this day my most fearful experiences at sea have come from other quarters.

Babs often speaks of her fear of **boarding a hove-to ship** in heavy weather. It stems from a radio call we once received from the passing oil-tanker *Kuaka*, querying our safety while we were jury steering in heavy weather north of Cape Palliser. Our anemometer had recently self-destructed, but we were told that it was gusting 87 knots at the ship's bridge. The radio operator audibly blanched when Babs responded that we were two adults with three small children, and proceeding under control. Babs' description of her view of the ship from the galley port-hole says it all. Through the scud and spume, a swaying bridge-deck towered above the elongated mass of white water which presumably indicated the location of its hull. "Even if we *had* been in genuine difficulties, there was *no way* I'd ever transfer in those circumstances!" she declares.

She goes on to describe her experience boarding a moving ship fourteen miles from the infamous Moruroa atoll. The New Zealand Navy vessel *HMNZS Tui* had invited her to come aboard with our two youngest children for a medical check-up and ice-creams, during our protest action outside the French nuclear test zone:

"We were ferried by zodiac to a rope ladder hanging near the stern. There was a four-metre swell running, so the ship was rolling heavily. We kept being sucked under the overhang, not far from the churn of the massive propeller. I was so terrified I could hardly climb! I nearly fainted before two strong sailors reached down and lifted me the last metre over the rail."

For me the fear of **fire afloat** is a serious one. So far I've been lucky, but I certainly felt the knotted stomach and dizzy panic late one night when acrid smoke reached my dozing nostrils. It was my inability to locate the source of this rapidly increasing menace that filled me with horror. As Babs roused our five sleeping boys and herded them up on deck my panic subsided sufficiently to remember the golden rule – isolate the batteries. Twenty minutes later, once the saloon had become habitable again, son number two confessed. He had patched some seriously undersized wires direct from the house battery bank to his transistor radio, using Sellotape for insulation and no fuse. Aaargh!

Even worse than fire is the threat of **explosion** aboard. When we switched from kerosene to LPG for cooking, decades ago, I took the precaution of paying a professional gas-fitter to install the copper gas-line. So it was definitely a stomach-churning experience to discover three days later that the 9kg gas bottle had alarmingly emptied during the three day passage to our South Island cruising ground. Soapy water soon revealed an internal leak that had been steadily filling our bilges, so we were living aboard a floating bomb. Watchers aboard the neighbouring boats on the Picton jetty must have seriously wondered if we were bonkers, with our chain-gang of children deployed for two hours emptying dozens of visibly empty buckets over the side.

Dark nights have been the catalyst for another of my greatest personal fears too: **fear of collision**. During the early coastal voyaging days aboard *New Zealand Maid*, we had hardly any of the electronic conveniences that now accompany our passage-making. It was panic-stations one particularly dark night when a loom appeared on the horizon directly ahead, comparable to the glow of a medium sized coastal town before bedtime. By the time I had double-checked my dead-reckoning it had already revealed itself as a mass of individual lights, row upon row, stacked in horizontal layers. This cruise ship was clearly approaching at considerable speed, and try as I might I could discern neither navigation lights nor range lights. Had it seen us? Did we present an adequate radar footprint? Would it pass to port or starboard? By now I had reached the vision-blurring state of serious concern, and began helming directly towards shore. The light from this monstrosity was rapidly destroying my night vision as it continued to bear down on our insignificant vessel with its precious young sleeping cargo. My ears were beginning to roar as I spun the helm to starboard, vainly searching among the mass of lights for any hint of red or green. It was a radio call from channel 16 that saved my sanity. *Royal Viking Star*'s second mate, observing my erratic course changes, had the decency to call and put me out of my misery, informing that he intended to pass five hundred metres to seaward of my current course, and apologising for the rather overwhelmed navigation lights. As the floating hotel rumbled past, I observed a hint of red among the dazzle near the bridge.

Without radar or AIS on our ketch until very recent years, our watchkeeping vigilance has sometimes approached paranoia over the risk of collision. One difficult night as we closed New Zealand's North Cape from the tropics has become permanently etched into my mind. Visibility was virtually non-existent in the torrential rain, and we were very aware that we were approaching shipping lanes – so much so that I had our spreader lights switched on all night to illuminate our sails and create a loom capable of being seen from a distance of half a football field. The half-hourly 'all ships' VHF call stating our position may have helped. At some point we heard a similar VHF call from *Melinda Lee*, an American sloop which had been our neighbour a few days earlier in Nukualofa.

It was not until after we had cleared customs three days later that the tragic news hit us. When a Taiwanese log ship had scored a direct hit on *Melinda Lee's* vulnerable hull during the small hours of that awful night, the family stood little chance. After their yacht and cute little boy disappeared under the waves less than a minute after the impact, it was only the mother who was able to resist fatal hypothermia as she huddled in her watchkeeping clothing with her scantily clad husband and daughter in their exposed inflatable dinghy. Two decades later, the shock of that incident still haunts me as I resist the temptation to sleep during the dog-watch hours.

However, it is the fear of less visible **floating hazards** that gives me even greater concern, various objects that drift awash and unlit. In daylight hours, logs and shipping containers are potentially visible but at night the chance of sightings is virtually zilch. As we trundle through the darkness on a moonless night-watch, it is our comprehensive contingency planning that keeps me from panic. On the *Maid* we have an assortment of semi-waterproof patching compounds and even a petrol fire-pump. We all have specifically allocated jobs in case of emergency. They may not prevent a crisis, but at least they provide a framework to overcome panic-stricken chaos.

I was aboard the aluminium cutter *Cachalot of Hobart* in early 2023 on a fairly wild night, closing Southport after a two-handed Tasman Sea crossing, when an All-Stations VHF call advised of a large drifting concrete pontoon. Its estimated position, approximately 20 miles north-east of Danger Point, lay slap-bang in our path as we careered towards the Queensland port.

With virtually zero visibility ahead, I spent my watch calculating the odds in our favour, after first loosening the life-raft straps!

This nightmare pontoon seems less menacing in a photo, published on social media the following day, in calmer weather.

IMPORTANT: Please beware of an old floating pontoon with a concrete base of about 5mtrs x 3mtrs in size drifting out at sea (last seen yesterday east of Currumbin in around 40 mtrs deep of water). You seriously wouldn't want to hit that and especially if it was dark or rough.

Two of our own sons once careered into a whale at eighteen knots under spinnaker during a trans-Tasman yacht race. They were aboard a plywood hard-chine sloop and Ben recounts seeing blood in the sea. His first reaction was to pull up a floorboard to check the bilge. His presence of mind in such an emergency astounds me. As a lesser mortal, I wonder whether the shock of such a dire incident would have rendered me useless. Meanwhile. below deck, lying in his off-watch bunk, seventeen-year-old Josh was literally too stunned to react. His head had been slammed into the bulkhead as *Whispers II* had come to an abrupt halt, and he was in a state of confusion rather than fear. Thankfully the hull survived, and the whale disappeared, hopefully to lick its wounds and live to tell the tale. But from that day hence, Josh has made a point of *always* sleeping with his feet forward while racing.

Our good friends Lisa and Horatio were crashing to windward between the Falklands and South Georgia on a typically wild night while their two young sons slept, when their 54ft cold-moulded wooden sloop crunched to a sudden halt. The culprit was almost certainly a growler, and the ingress of very cold seawater was immediate. They are wry about it in the telling, but I can only begin to imagine the sheer desperation of their situation. That cold hand of icy fear that must have gripped them both as they clawed at the joinery to internally access the damaged hull. It was a tale of courage and sheer determination that luckily had a satisfactory ending, but many is the vessel that has disappeared without trace during my sailing lifetime after meeting a similar but less successful outcome.

Ice generates a fear of its own. I have spent a little time in ice-strewn waters – enough to respect and fear the stuff. It comes in many variables. Certainly growlers and bergy bits come in the same category as uncharted rocks, with watchkeeping vigilance to match the risk. Pack ice behaves like a logjam with the added property of potentially fusing together to create a permanent icefield. Picking our way through pack ice aboard *Snow Petrel*, we were very aware that our leads were not quite like a typical shore channel. Our greatest fear was that once we had worked our way into the heart of the pack, our inbound channel would close behind us and squeeze us like a nutcracker. Even when we were clear of the pack, ice presented an additional fear, when 100 knot winds began whipping seawater through our rigging. The rapid build-up of ice aloft had the potential mass to counterbalance the weight of our keel. Capsize in subzero water has no happy ending; as befell the unfortunate crew of *Berserk II* in Antarctica's Ross Sea in one violent storm.

*Ice build-up in **Snow Petrel's** rigging, during an Antarctic blizzard.*

Fear of the unknown is something that we are all vulnerable to. We can be rational about explicable matters, but when something spooks us, the heart-stopping reaction kicks in. While I don't particularly believe in sea monsters, I was embarrassingly caught out one twilight aboard the fishing ketch *Sunniva* in the Tasman Sea, shortly before we retrieved our tuna lures for the night. Glancing astern in the twilit gloom, my eye fixated on a ghastly tentacle swaying above the oily sea like a six-foot cobra performing for a snake charmer. As I watched, mesmerised, it flopped onto the surface with a slap, then lazily rose and swayed, as if somehow surveying our lonely vessel with evil intent. In my state of stunned horror, it took a seeming eternity before my dry mouth was capable of calling my sole companion on deck to help stave off this monstrosity.

"Wow – don't very often see a thresher shark out here!" he commented, squinting through the fading light. "Big one too! He's after our lures. Thinks they're a school of pilchards." As we watched, the tentacle betrayed itself as something more blade-like in shape, and the slaps became more insistent. Clearly this big daddy was becoming frustrated that his normal fish-stunning tail slap wasn't having its usual impact on our school of lures.

Thresher shark

The same gut-wrenching fear of the unknown is prone to catch us unaware during lonely night watches too. I well recall a night in *Snow Petrel*'s cockpit, ghosting along quietly under full canvas under the stars, comfortably minding my own business, when I became abruptly aware of a massive blue phosphorescent glow emerging rapidly from the depths near our starboard quarter. It was the unexpectedness and sheer size of this shapeless apparition that sent my heart into my mouth and kept me riveted to the rail until he burst to the surface barely two metres away– his massive head and tiny eye backlit by the blue phosphorescence that he had churned up during his dramatic entrance. Fear was replaced by fascination as he hung there – the familiar *pfffff* accompanied by a whoosh of bad breath – before he slid quietly back into his personal blue glow and swirled away, doubtless in search of a more amenable fin whale cow to pay him the attention he deserved. These incidents seem trivial compared to Australian Mike Thurston's almost unbelievable double-whammy scare-to-beat-all-scares in 2018. His 50 ft aluminium ketch *Drina* was en route to Capetown from South Georgia on 18th January, 2018 (Noon Position: 44° 13' S, 13° 19'W), comfortably running down the roaring Forties minding her own business. Shortly after sunset a sudden lurch heralded the jaw-dropping adrenaline-pumping sight of a massive squid attaching itself to the foredeck with flailing tentacles and suckers the size of dinner-plates. By the time Mike and his crew had gathered their wits, dodging the huge razor-sharp beak in their vain attempts to prise it loose with boat-hooks, its tentacles had taken a firm grasp of the standing rigging to the lower spreaders. By now the sheer weight of this kraken was threatening to capsize the ketch, already low on her marks and listing heavily.

As if their hearts weren't already beating overtime, there came a second – more violent - lurch followed by the unmistakeable head and gaping jaw of an enormous sperm whale exploding out of the sea alongside and clamping onto a couple of flailing tentacles. Mike recounts somewhat understatedly that "...the tussle that ensued was mesmerizing, but we were obliged to crowd on more sail to gain sea-room as quickly as possible from the battling leviathans." In similar circumstances I rather suspect that I would be likewise beating a hasty heart-in-mouth retreat.

As *Drina* opened up a respectable distance from the churning water, the mighty jaw severed two flailing tentacles as the massive beak slashed a huge gash into the whale's head. Mouths agape, *Drina*'s crew witnessed a violent death-roll just as a huge wave of black ink erupted from the desperate squid. The last view, as *Drina* sped away, was of an oily black slick spreading over the churning water as the monsters disappeared beneath the surface.

This is the stuff of legends. Rough weather - pah! For an ultimate fear, this one certainly takes the podium.

***

Kraken *engraved by W H Lizars, 1839*
(R.Hamilton, The Naturalists Library)

12

The Mince Tart Voyage.

By 2016 Babs and I had itchy feet again. It was time to leave Tasmania and spend some time on a leisurely cruise around New Zealand again.

My father was once asked if it was possible to walk between Australia and New Zealand at low tide. Apparently it was a serious question from an American who clearly had little knowledge of either geography or tides. It generally takes us at least eight days to cross the Tasman at a steady jog, so I figure it would have to be a mighty long low tide, notwithstanding a 4000 metre inter-tidal range.

Until now, if anyone had proposed sailing between Australia and New Zealand's southern-most customs ports two weeks before the mid-winter solstice, Babs and I would have seriously questioned their sanity. Sane sailors don't generally pop across this stretch of ocean, south of the 45th parallel, at this time of year. The proof was in the pudding – not a single other AIS signal to be seen from Storm Bay to Foveaux Strait. Yet there we were, sailing *New Zealand Maid* past Fiordland's snow-capped peaks in the splendid company of albatrosses, prions and petrels as the Bluff fisherfolk were scraping the frost off their 'winderscreens'.

It wasn't originally meant to happen like this. I'd proposed a nice little jaunt across from Hobart to Enzed at around the equinox, in a comfortable patch of settled weather and of course a full moon to light up our night watches. However, as always, things got in the way: Matt's Bruny Island wedding, storing the inevitable clutter of our decade's sojourn in Tasmania, an ever-expanding list of re-fit jobs on *New Zealand Maid*.... Before we knew it, winter was nearly upon us with a parade of Cold Fronts to taunt us. When at last the promise of a slow-moving blocking High appeared on the meteorological horizon, Babs and I abandoned our list and resolved to seize the moment. It was a great concept, stock the *Maid* up with diesel and ride a High across the whole way, for a Gentleman's Passage to NZ. Our eldest son Ben was not impressed. In his view we needed to shake down the *Maid* to sort out potential glitches in all the electrical, mechanical and rigging work we had recently been doing. As a teacher of shipboard safety and navigation he knew what he was talking about. But Babs and I were sick of the lists and the ceaseless preparation. We were grateful when he eventually relented and offered to sail with us. It would be his eleventh

Tasman crossing under sail, far more than our combined total. With Ben, Dan and Matt pitching in to help during the final days, things moved fast.

The great thing about Ben is that he's the ultimate package for this sort of voyage. Square rig officer, Antarctic skipper, walking maritime encyclopaedia and techno-buff all rolled into one. He could teach us to drive the new four-year-old radar/plotter, set up handy-billies and share the night watches. It would compensate for all his lectures about how silly we were being.

 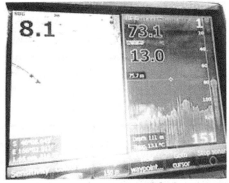

Ben is the ultimate package!　　　*Our new four-year-old plotter*

We all decided that this passage had to be named 'The Mince Tart Voyage'. The reason was simple. Our final act in the last sleepless night of provisioning had been to empty our Bruny Island freezer and load its contents aboard for the trip. (This would mean eating our way through rather a lot of meat – anything remaining would be destroyed by NZ Quarantine officials on arrival.) And there at the very bottom of the freezer was a glorious discovery – five dozen fruit-mince tarts which had been squirrelled away at Christmas for winter treats. Coupled with the 3 kg fruit cake our friends Kim and Tony had already given us, night watches were to become rather gluttonous.

Tasman Sea crossing　　　*Fruit mince tarts – delicious.*

The concept of setting sail in the midst of a slow-moving high-pressure system sounds good on paper. We pored over the various 10-day weather models and being an optimist, I chose to ignore the one with the bad weather behind the system. We filled the tanks with diesel, along with seven 20 litre jerry-cans. Enough fuel for 750 miles of motoring. Simple !

There is a flaw to this concept though. It became more obvious on our third night out, as we struggled with a faulty auto-pilot. The HF radio began issuing storm-warnings for the Australian and Tasmanian coasts behind us. We would have to keep moving within the bubble of east-moving high pressure to avoid being caught in the squash zone behind it. But with very little wind we were being forced to use up our fuel reserves. With 1150 miles to Nelson (equivalent of Scotland to Greenland), we would be a sitting duck when the fuel ran out – wallowing in a light headwind that would rapidly become a head-gale.

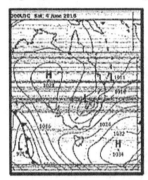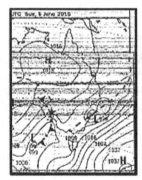

The weather faxes showed our anticyclone out-running us.

Ben's proposal was one that Babs and I had joked heartily about weeks earlier when a computer model suggested it: alter course for the southern tip of NZ, to the customs port of Bluff - as there are no clearance ports on the South Island's west coast. At a mere 950 miles on the rhumb line, this would save us two days and reduce the diesel deficit. Already radio reports were announcing carnage and significant loss of life behind us in Australia. Talking to our live-aboard neighbour via our new twenty-year-old Codan HF radio, we learned that our Tasmanian marina pier had

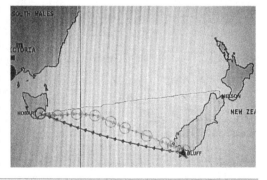

just snapped in half! A course alteration really was a no-brainer, despite ending up some 600 miles from our intended destination. Once we had become used to the idea, we settled down to thoroughly enjoy the trip. Babs cooked up a succession of wonderful meals, doing her best to consume anything that would be snaffled by NZ quarantine officials on arrival. We motor-sailed through gentle seas whilst completing some of the tasks left on the List, even a little joinery and rigging work. We became masters at the art of power-assisted sailing, setting six sails and using an idling engine to draw the gentle following breeze forward of our beam. This would bring the log up to a wonderful six-plus knots while the engine merely sipped at the fuel.

Puysegur Point at the southern tip of Fiordland has a particularly nasty reputation and obliged us by freshening the NE breeze to a welcome 25 knots as we approached, guaranteeing the survival of our remaining two cans of diesel, and dipping the lee rail briefly for a deck-wash. With a storm warning announced for this patch of water next day, we were particularly pleased to see the log climb to eight knots.

A welcome breeze at last.

The last time Babs and I had visited Bluff was to hitch a ride to Antarctica for hut maintenance work, aboard the Russian icebreaker *Akademik Shokalskiy* on her infamous 2014/15 debacle voyage. This time, inward bound with the flood tide, we were reminded a little of Antarctica, with ice still encrusting the wharf as we docked. It was eight days to the very hour since our departure – probably our slowest trans-Tasman but certainly our most sedate. And ahead of us was the unusual but very welcome prospect of a brief Stewart Island cruise before farewelling Ben and wandering up the East Coast to Nelson.

Believe it or not, there were still a dozen mince tarts in the starboard locker for those north-bound night watches.

***

13

Cruising Earthquake Waters

(Five months after the Mince Tart voyage, Babs and I were enjoying cruising our old stamping ground when our world turned topsy turvy.)

Feeling our way into a secluded Queen Charlotte Sound cove, we watch the sounder nervously. A month ago we cruised in here boldly, secure in the knowledge that our charts were as accurate as modern technology could allow. Today things are different. To starboard, well into the cove, a pale green shadow-line and two protruding branches betray a fresh underwater danger. As I ease the anchor past the bobstay and release the windlass, I survey a dirt-yellow scar which has slashed its way down the hillside, and the tangle of roots and trunks littering the shoreline at its base. We are both very aware that it took only ninety seconds last week for one dramatic tectonic upheaval to shatter our complacency in these waters. We have been warned of underwater mudslides which have already ruined the holding in other formerly secure anchorages. We wait to see if the anchor will bite.

*

We were caught ashore, visiting Babs' parents overnight, when the powerful 7.8 magnitude Kaikoura quake occurred. The evidence was on their clock next morning in Nelson, ninety miles from the epicentre. The pendulum had lost its rhythm at precisely two minutes past midnight, as the power lines outside began shorting in a shower of sparks. Had it occurred ten hours later, we would have been back aboard *New Zealand Maid*'s mooring near Picton, significantly closer to the epicentre.

Several anxious aftershock-ridden hours later, the news began to flow. Images of collapsed shopfronts in Picton, along with evacuations from many residences near our mooring, flashed across the TV screen among even more spectacular visuals from various other locations. A tsunami scare had most low-lying coastal residents on tenterhooks. In both Picton and Wellington harbours the ferry terminals were no longer functioning, due (it was later rumoured) to these ships abandoning their berths in haste whilst still attached to the massive passenger corridors.

We cursed ourselves at our bad luck in being separated from our floating home during such a crisis. Had we been aboard, at least we would have had the option of motoring her out into Queen Charlotte Sound's deeper water. But for now she was at the mercy of the elements. We were cut off from Picton, with all roads between us and her mooring impassable. Nearer the epicentre, whole hillsides had swallowed up the road and rail arterial routes. Bridge approaches had become displaced vertically, and chasms had appeared across stretches of tar seal. During the two day wait for slips to be sufficiently cleared and

The epicentre was north of Kaikoura

detours established, our imaginations ran riot. But eventually we saw her, our beautiful black ketch, lying serenely at her mooring as if nothing extraordinary had bothered her during her time alone.

We were certainly pleased to have hauled our dinghy well above the shingle beach, but our fears of a tsunami sweeping this landlocked arm of the sound had been groundless. True the beach had altered shape somewhat, with a rocky layer scoured clear of gravel, but we had not been affected in the way that Pigeon Bay, on the more exposed Banks Peninsula further south had been, with a house washed clean off its foundations.

The original shoreline (left) was now inland, with new reefs exposed to seaward.

Understandably, the news reports had all been focusing on the land-based infrastructure damage which had occurred. But we were abruptly reminded that, as mariners, we were about to be faced with a different set of challenges when we switched on our VHF and were greeted with a barrage of coastal navigation warnings. The first was ominous enough: *Following earthquake activity, mariners are warned that aids to navigation may be unreliable and there may be unusual tides.* The second warning was also disturbing: *Mariners are warned that charted depths may have changed in sea-areas Conway, Cook and Castlepoint.* Clearly, for the immediate future at least, we water-dwellers were going to have to revert to 'number one eyeball' navigation.

The authorities had quite reasonably diverted their energies towards making good the essentials of life to various stricken land-based communities. Helicopters and naval vessels were too busy to be checking whether beacons and lighthouses had collapsed into the sea. Luckily one sharp-eyed skipper was quick to report the disappearance of the beacon at Keep Clear Rock, half a mile out from Danger Point, in time to publicise the fact before it could claim a victim. Meanwhile many less advertised dangers lurked, such as the dozens of huge logs which had been sucked into the waterways to lie semi-submerged in wait for the unwary.

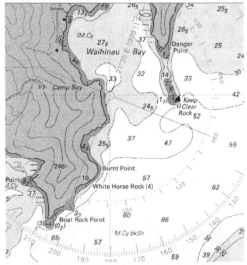

Keep Clear Rock beacon disappeared.

Then there were the 'unusual tides' - a more alarming phenomenon than might be expected, as they are second-cousins of the tsunami. Tide tables had become unreliable until the aftershocks had subsided and the sea began breathing normally once again. The enclosed waterways of the Marlborough Sounds, which are a maze of bush-clad drowned valleys full of reaches and islands, are interspersed with occasional narrow passes. We always plan our cruising around the tides, because a three or four knot current can lengthen or shorten a half-day passage by some hours. The most critical two passes are French Pass and Tory Channel, where currents reach up to seven knots. As an immediate precaution, the Cook Strait entrance to Tory Channel was declared off-limits to all craft until the ebb and flow returned to its predictable schedules. For the meantime, Babs and I had no intention of venturing into questionable locations. We were happy enough to simply potter for a week or three around the inner Queen Charlotte inlets, checking out the condition of favourite anchorages. However extra precautions were even necessary when leaving our dinghy ashore. We had previously experienced a four-foot rise and fall at twenty-minute intervals in Tasmania after the catastrophic 2004 Sumatra tsunami.

For most New Zealanders (and indeed most mariners who sail around the Pacific rim), earthquakes are a fact of life. They are a random threat with which we live in the knowledge that we are spared many of the stresses found in other parts of the world – snakes, poisonous insects, wildfires, over-population and nightmare politicians.

The 'rim of fire', as it is known, is renowned for its unstable coastlines where massive tectonic plates constantly do battle. But of all its zones, New Zealand takes the podium for variety. In the far south, the west coast is moving steadily north in relation to the east coast. Further north, the seafloor off the east coast is driving steadily under the North Island, pushing its coastline ever upwards. In central New Zealand, where we are currently cruising near Cook Strait, both are happening simultaneously. This is where the issue of altered charted depths comes into play. As I write weeks later, our VHF is transmitting instructions to keep clear of a government survey vessel which is assessing our seafloor. The coastline to the east of the faultline has definitely risen by ten feet in places, creating beaches and platforms some distance beyond the former charted shoreline.

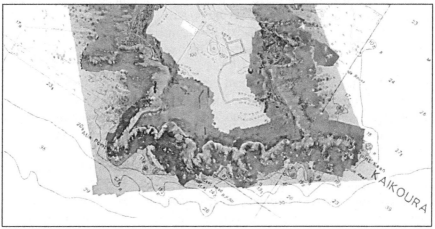

Re-surveying near the altered Kaikoura shoreline for altered depths.

Locals had a great time plucking hundreds of stranded crayfish and paua (abalone) along the coastline. The whale-watching charter vessels at Kaikoura became instantly landlocked, to remain so until a million-dollar channel could be blasted out of the raised intertidal coastal platform. However for those of us on the west side of the faultline there was fortunately nothing so dramatic. Perhaps the new survey would reveal newly exposed rocks or maybe even that our Sounds' coast-scape had subsided. Only time would tell.

The biggest potential danger to any vessel moored or anchored near a Pacific-rim coast is the tsunami. Offshore, where these beasts run low and fast (up to 600mph), they can pass unnoticed, but near shoaling coastlines where they metamorphose into a huge scale tidal bore, there is little that can withstand them. Luckily for *New Zealand Maid*, the epicentre of our Kaikoura quake, being inshore, had failed to trigger a seafloor upthrust like the 9.1 magnitude 2004 Sumatran event, which killed a quarter of a million people. A Tasmanian cruising couple were anchored outside the regular breaker line off Thailand's Phuket resort during the preliminary surge, and were savvy enough to instantly cut loose their anchor and begin steaming into deeper water over ten fathoms. They showed us a photo that they were later given, which clearly shows their 38ft sloop rearing to the point of near-pitchpole as it breasted the vertical face of the principal tsunami, while a number of less prepared yachts further inshore are being swept beam-on to their doom.

Our son Ben also narrowly avoided the destruction of an extreme seafloor megathrust. He had been on the Japanese east coast near Fukushima only ten days before the notorious 2011 tsunami, preparing a 110ft workboat for delivery to Australia. The battered hull was later found over 4 miles inland.

Despite the fact that we had dodged a significant tsunami, we did notice plenty of seiche action in the Marlborough Sounds, which accounted for the large numbers of drifting logs. A seiche is a less-famous first-cousin of the tsunami, being essentially the sloshing action that occurs when enclosed waters are stirred up. For example, the 8.2 magnitude 1855 Wellington quake saw huge waves rushing from side to side of the five-mile diameter harbour like water in a washing bowl. Wharves and buildings were destroyed, ships were grounded and re-floated at regular intervals, and a huge bore raced up the Hutt River, destroying any bridges in its path. Wellington is currently overdue for another big one, and during the seven years we intermittently lived aboard there we were nervously conscious of our vulnerability, tethered to the top of 40-foot mooring-poles which swayed like treetops during every random tremor. Our prime contingency plan in the event of a major seismic disturbance was to cast off and make for the central harbour. And (we told our boys) put on a lifejacket!

I have lived through a few rather alarming earthquakes during my time on this planet, but I have so far dodged a major bullet. *New Zealand Maid* was once high and dry in our backyard when a moderate local quake rattled us, dislodging five of the seven wooden props from under her garboards. (My life might have been very different if the last two had dropped out.)

Despite all these potential hazards, if we sailors lived in fear of nature's forces, we wouldn't go to sea. The chances of being wrecked by tectonic misadventure are considerably less than the dangers of meteorological events, which in turn pose statistically far less risk than being mown down by an out-of-control truck! Cruising the earthquake prone rim of fire has its own advantages. Excuse me now while I pop up on deck to view the stars and breathe our pristine air. The anchor has held, and those protruding branches to starboard have gathered some streamers of weed. Above me near the scarred hillside, a morepork owl is hooting. Perhaps it is telling me that all is still as nature intended.

Moored near an earthquake scarred hillside..

14

Transiting Panama

(Two years later we were off voyaging again on a very different yacht, leaving the Maid behind in New Zealand.)

The jungle has closed around us, so much so that in the taxi headlights, only a single-laned crumbling road is visible. Barely an hour earlier our taxi had been driving between the skyscrapers of Panama City and along a four-laned motorway. But that was before the car-ferry ride across the canal into Panama's unsanitised alter-ego landscape. Now, as the driver swerves to avoid one of hundreds of crater-sized pot-holes, Babs glances apprehensively at our packs, loaded with equipment for our forthcoming 4000 mile passage to Tahiti. But I am confident enough that our Panamanian driver has no sinister intentions.

Panama is certainly a land of contrasts. As a child, I imagined a flattish countryside surrounding a tidily straight canal stretching between two oceans. Neither jungles nor skyscrapers were part of this image. But life has a way of putting such naïve images into perspective.

It is barely a fortnight since we answered an email from son Josh, eager for us to join him and Sara aboard the 50ft *Rogue* that they had sailed to the Caribbean from France. With our three liveliest grandsons aboard, we suspect that our roles will involve correspondence schoolwork as well as spreading the night-watch duties during the 4000-mile leg to French Polynesia. Already this is proving to be one of those unexpected adventures that have punctuated our lives for decades.

Rogue in Los Perlos Islands

In a mixture of puzzlement and relief, we pull up at an armed checkpoint, the barrier arm stretching between 3-metre-high razor-wire tipped walls which continue into darkened jungle on either side. After a brief staccato exchange of unintelligible conversation, we are through, deeper into the dense, bamboo-lined jungle.

Abruptly, ten minutes later, a glimmer of light gives way to a scene of relative familiarity. A forest of masts becomes visible behind a small cluster of whitewashed Spanish-style buildings. We have arrived at Shelter Bay Marina – an unexpected oasis of relative familiarity in this country of contrasts.

It doesn't take many days to discover the distinctive dynamic of this unusual marina – it certainly rates as a particularly fun-filled community of transients and locals. The conversation-opener here invariably centres on '*The Queue*', and what date had been allotted for each vessel's transit through the canal. It is now late April, and rumour has it that there is at least a fortnight's delay after the measuring protocols before any likelihood of a transit date. Two weeks seems a very long time for us new arrivals, struggling to acclimatise to the sticky heat on top of groggy jet-lag. It doesn't take long to discover why our three grandsons spend so much time in the 2-star swimming pool close to *Rogue*'s marina pier.

The adventure has barely begun, and we are fascinated by the local jungle-life. Someone warns the boys of a hungry local Black Caiman (alligatorid crocodilian) that frequents the muddy creek not far from the swimming pool. Two days later it is sighted, like a semi-submerged three metre log, cruising through the marina barely three boat-lengths past *Rogue*'s stern. Shortly after, adding to the mystique, the surrounding jungle begins to emit a series of chilling roars, which we initially assume to be a jaguar until someone casually identifies the source as a troop of Howler Monkeys.

Rogue hauled out.   *The jungle ruins of Fort Sherman*

Days pass. We do our best to help bring the boys' correspondence schoolwork up to date in the air-conditioned coolness of the second-floor lounge of the aging ex-army building nearby. Our transit date is confirmed. Josh arranges for *Rogue* to be lifted out for two days – sufficient for a quick scrub and antifoul in the shade of two tall coconut palms as well as a check of the rudder bearing. For diversions we take the boys to explore nearby jungle tracks, and discover the nearby overgrown ruins of the century-old American military batteries. Formerly Fort Sherman, the massive concrete structures and tunnels have been almost completely reclaimed by the jungle during the past forty years, with dozens of busy leaf-cutter ant trails replacing the former bustle of jeeps and heavy equipment. Both Josh and Sara opt to do the transit as line-handlers for other yachts. It is a common diversion, which helps familiarise first-timers with the canal and its demands. Arrangements for the transit are made by an agent (it would be virtually impossible without one). A date and time is allotted, as well as a partner sailing vessel. Skippers must declare a cruising speed, to help with the pairing, as well as to match yacht pairs with a suitable ship which will share the locks. Each yacht is also allocated an 'advisor' (pilot in training) to guide the skipper through the more difficult aspects of the canal.

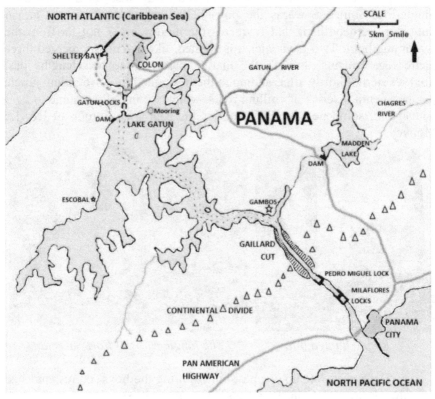

Our day finally arrives, and we say our farewells to new friends who are days behind us in the queue. To my delight we have been allocated a 1500 hr commencement, which will see us 'locked' up into Lake Gatun during late afternoon in the company of a tanker and similar-sized yacht. We will then be spending a night lashed alongside a giant mooring buoy in the lake, 26 metres above sea-level with our partner yacht (a 50 ft cat from Oregon USA). No transiting is allowed during hours of darkness, so the alternative would have been an early 0500 start to cover the entire distance in a single day.

It is an exciting and rather hair-raising experience as we enter the first of the three Gatun locks at the Caribbean end of the canal. On either side of us, the darkened concrete walls tower nearly three storeys upwards. We are directed toward the front of the lock, securely rafted to our American buddy catamaran *Baloo*, and thrown a pair of heaving lines – one for our port bow and the other to me at the port aft cleat. Our immediate job is to secure these to our own rented set of lengthy heavy mooring lines, for retrieval by the Panamanian line-handlers high above us. While this is happening, we are almost too busy to notice the same procedure happening aboard *Baloo*'s port side, and a giant tanker being towed into the lock astern of us by a pair of locomotives.

The rear lock-gate closes and we wait in anticipation. Suddenly the water is boiling and surging violently around us. My job is to take up the slack on the aft line as we rapidly rise. The ladder rungs on the lock wall, only metres to my left, are disappearing at ten second intervals, but I'm working too hard on the winch to pay much attention. We are at the mercy of *Baloo*'s crew working the starboard lines – too much slack could see *Rogue* crunching the lock wall. I'm very conscious of my own responsibility, as any inattention

Water boils and surges around us.

could see *Baloo* crunching the opposite wall. Raised voices and tension fill the air, until I'm suddenly aware of a view ahead over an almost submerged lock gate. The massive lock-walls have nearly disappeared underwater, and the gates ahead are already opening in a swirl of water. Ahead the locomotive tracks rise abruptly, and we are motioned forward into a second similar lock, our Panamanian linesmen jogging alongside with our lines.

By the time we have been raised through the third lock we are becoming more confident. Ahead is a huge spread of water, punctuated by random shipping – some stationary – as well as a scatter of islands and channel markers. Our adviser instructs us to unlash from *Baloo* and proceed for a couple of miles along this lake edge to the mooring which will be our overnight location. On arrival this turns out to be a massive rubber-ringed floating disc, some four metres in diameter, which we are instructed to lash firmly amidships to port, while *Baloo* follows suit on the opposite side. Without waiting to inspect the final spiderweb of spring-lines, our adviser leaps aboard a fast-moving pilot-vessel and is off, shouting instructions in faltering English to be ready for departure by 0730.

It becomes a rather social evening, rafted on this giant mooring. Floating in fresh water for the first time in her existence, *Rogue* has settled a little below her marks. The mosquitoes aren't as persistent as we had feared, and in the quiet dawn we climb from our bunks eager to continue this unusual adventure.

Lake Gatun mooring

Sunrise on the lake brings reflections and a welcome coolness. Lake Gatun is an artificially enlarged body of water, created by drowning an inland river system. Several ships lie on anchor a mile or two distant, and a couple are underway towards yesterday's locks. We have scarcely finished our hasty breakfast when the workboat carves its way through the stillness, disgorging two fresh advisers onto *Baloo* and *Rogue*. A flurry of activity after some brief introductions, and we cast off - backtracking towards the first red post that will lead us into the broad deep shipping channel for the next 20 miles.

For the grandkids, boredom soon sets in as we motor steadily for the first couple of hours across the wide expanse of water, but as we

sweep close past the jungle-clad shoreline of Barro Colorado Island all eyes are peeled for monkeys and alligators, while a couple of brightly coloured parrots flap past. An hour later and the lake narrows, betraying its drowned valley origins. Occasionally a covered dory buzzes across the channel, ferrying locals between obscured villages near the lake margins. To our port we become aware of a railway line as we munch into sandwiches and the adviser chats in heavily accented English. In the distance ahead, a distinctly man-made landscape is emerging, with impressively terraced hillsides stepping down on either side into a narrowing channel. Our pilot adviser sweeps his arm towards the terracing, "Gaillard Cut", he announces proudly.

Gaillard Cut - an engineering wonder

To both sides of us now is growing evidence of the huge mechanical effort involved in the construction and maintenance of this famous waterway. Rusting remains of old machinery litter the shoreline, while on the hillsides, curious pipelines and raised structures give an indication of the past and present effort required to build and maintain the canal. We hug the eastern bank to reduce the wash from a deep-laden passing tanker, and I study the chart in curiosity.

We have now completed three-quarters of our journey between the Atlantic and Pacific, and this cutting is bringing us through the watershed of the great continental divide, a shortcut which has saved the canal-builders several sets of docks during construction.

Another hour, and we are approaching the first of our 'downhill' locks, the routine of preparing raft-up lines to *Baloo* once more. This process is old hat now, but the experience of locking downwards is a new one, and the four of us line-handlers struggle to coordinate as the water level drops at an alarming speed. Our adviser doesn't help our stress levels as he recounts how, only a few days earlier, a line had jammed aboard a catamaran in this lock, slamming it against the concrete wall before tearing a huge cleat clean out of its deck. By the time we reach the second and third locks, twenty minutes later we are better prepared, watched by dozens of sightseers from the vantage of a viewing platform barely fifty metres away.

As the final massive gate swings open, we are unmistakeably at sea-level, the channel widening towards a view of open sea studded with waiting ships and a skyline of high-rise buildings to port. The Pacific is about to greet us with a spectacular thunderstorm, but nobody cares. Champagne flows as the three youngsters prance excitedly in the cockpit. For these boys the excitement of returning to their home ocean is a memory they will carry for the rest of their lives. And for Babs and I, the ancient mariners of the crew, another piece of the giant jigsaw puzzle that constitutes human endeavour on our watery planet, has been revealed.

The skyline of Panama City emerges through a tropical cloudburst.

***

15

A Few Islands...

One of the conversation starters, over a rum or three at voyage end, is often a discussion about the most unusual landfalls. Babs and I have a personal stock which mostly entails remote islands.

Cocos Island, 2018:

It was a spectacular landfall! Rising almost sheer from the equatorial Pacific, waterfalls cascaded down the rock faces, surrounded by a green lushness which we had not seen since leaving Panama a week earlier aboard *Rogue*. The opening sequences of 'Jurassic Park' give a helicopter-eye view of this spectacular jungle-clad island, but in our case it was a rather more sedate arrival, tentatively calling on Channel 16 for permission to briefly anchor to repair a mast-head light.

We were later to realise that none of the year's cohort of Pacific skippers had any idea of the existence or location of this former pirate island that we had randomly decided to visit en route to French Polynesia. They had mostly disregarded the need for any wide scale paper charts. Josh had chosen to make some westing north of the rhumb in an effort to avoid the widest zone of doldrums, and Babs and I, being 'old school' navigators, had brought some of our paper charts. The slightly battered chart of this part of the Pacific had identified a tiny blip north of the equator as Cocos Island, and we had logged it as a potential destination. To find it on a chart-plotter would be rather like hunting for a needle in a haystack, as any little blip will simply disappear on a vector chart unless magnified within a tiny rectangle.

In hindsight we were rash to be venturing inside this hundred-mile diameter Costa-Rican marine park without a permit. We were later to learn that formalities for visiting this remote island usually entail a four week visit to San Jose and the payment of a considerable sum of money. Our VHF call was answered in halting English with a heavy Spanish accent. We were not to anchor, and must proceed to the sheltered western bay onto the single empty mooring to await an interrogation from the island's rangers.

On arrival, the only vessel in sight was a battered blue 40ft steel ex-fishing-boat with an ominous machine-gun mounted on the foredeck. We waited rather apprehensively as an inflatable with five uniformed men launched from the beach and came alongside.

Fortunately we had the universal 'get-out-of jail-free' card aboard in the form of our three enthusiastic blonde sun-tanned grandsons. The rather grim demeanour of these men melted at the sight of these boys, and the two English-speaking rangers soon seemed happy enough to photograph our passports and fill in a single-page Spanish document. After a brief unintelligible conversion with their colleagues, to our relieved surprise, we were invited ashore.

In halting English, it emerged that we were the first foreign-flagged vessel to visit the island for four years! The half-dozen resident rangers are tasked with 'discouraging' long-line poachers from venturing inside the hundred-mile exclusion zone of the marine park with the help of that rather daunting foredeck weapon. These men spend alternate months tag-teaming a presence on the island and confiscating a massive shed-full of longlines from would-be poachers. It was revealed that they missed having their own children around, and that our youngsters were the first to set foot on Cocos for a considerable time.

The only vessels generally permitted to visit this marine park are Puerto Rican dive charter vessels, making the occasional 400-mile trip out from Puerto Rico. The last such expensive visit, a month or two earlier, had inconveniently lost a guest when he became dinner for a largish tiger shark, and we were warned under no circumstances to go swimming in the anchorage.

Waterfalls cascaded down lush green rock faces.

The anchor light was an easy fix - just a broken bulb. Peals of thunder began rolling around the steep volcanic rockfaces not long after we set foot ashore. Our three youngsters were immediately taken under the wings of our new friends, and we ducked for cover as the skies opened. A high island like this near the intertropical convergence is a sitting duck for impromptu storms, and we became a little anxious to get offshore before nightfall, despite an invitation to join the ranger team for an evening barbecue.

We spent sufficient time ashore to learn of the multiple legends of nineteenth century pirate treasure – billions of dollars in Spanish gold – which supposedly still lies buried in unknown locations about the nine square miles of volcanic soil. Whalers and slavers were also regular visitors in that century, collecting coconuts and water, as well as abandoning diseased slaves. Life was tough back then!

Our take-away from this unique experience was a philosophical one. If a third-world central American country is prepared to outlay considerable resources to preserve the integrity of a marine reserve of this magnitude, surely more first-world nations should do more to create reserves within their economic zones, instead of pandering to the corporate greed of their fishing lobbies. But maybe I'm just a naïve old gaffer.

MacKellar Islets, 2014:

Barely two miles north of Cape Denison in remote East Antarctica lie a group of islets known as the MacKellars. This location is officially the windiest location on the planet, and there is no record of any human visit to these islets since 1912 when members of Sir Douglas Mawson's heroic era science team ice-walked to them during a rare calm day in the early winter months in search of penguins for the pot. Tantalisingly close to the tiny boat harbour adjacent to Mawson's historic huts at Cape Denison, I was twice tempted to visit these before caution intervened. The first temptation occurred in 2006 when I sailed down from Tasmania aboard our son Ben's 34-ft *Snow Petrel*. The location is infamous for its sudden vicious katabatic gales often exceeding 100 knots, so with only a battered inflatable and ancient 2HP outboard, to claw our way back against a random southerly blizzard, we reluctantly deemed it rather foolhardy to potter across for a peek.

Two years later I was back, having hitched down aboard a French icebreaker with a small team to build a field hut. This time I was in possession of a 9 ft inflatable and a pair of oars for the sole purpose of sinking a tide-gauge into the bottom of the tiny inlet after the ice had broken out. Once again, the MacKellars beckoned; however as the explicit instructions from the Australian Antarctic Division authorities included a clause banning any other usage of my little blow-up, the temptation was once again curtailed.

The snow-capped MacKellar Islands lie tantalizingly close on a rare fine day, with grounded icebergs beyond. **Snow Petrel** *sits on anchor in boat harbour and Mawson's huts can be seen in the right foreground.*

My chance was finally to come six years later, having made the passage south aboard the icebreaker *Akademik Shokalskiy* to carry out some hut maintenance. Our little team disembarked with a pair of eight-wheel beach-buggies at the ice edge, rather inconveniently situated about forty miles offshore. On the flip side, our brief this time included the possibility that 'if time and conditions allowed' two of us had permission to venture over ice to the MacKellar Islets and conduct a ball-park tally of Adele penguin nests.

It was somewhat anticlimactic to park our Argo beach-buggy alongside Greater MacKellar Islet on a rare calm Antarctic endless day. The icy rock surface - unsurprisingly devoid of any hint of vegetation - was littered with abandoned penguin nests, some containing stone-cold eggs and others revealing fluffy corpses of abandoned fledgelings. Out on the vast white plain of fast ice behind us, dozens of dejected and confused adult penguins were waddling in search of a hopeful ice-edge for their krill dinner, some pausing to dive into knee-deep ponds of ice-melt on the surface of the fast-ice.

Finally at Greater McKellar Islet, after navigating over ice.

It is a sobering experience to venture to a location like this where virtually no humans have ever set foot, particularly in circumstances where an environmental disaster has upset the balance of nature in this tragic manner. However on a brighter note, Adele penguins are known to live for up to two decades, mating for life, so the colony was unlikely doomed to fail in the long term. During the four-year period that the megaberg B09B lay grounded off Cape Denison, all breeding at Cape Denison and the MacKellars was effectively halted. Chances are with global warming that more colossal chunks of the Ross Sea shelf will break away causing similar disasters, however satellite pictures in recent years reveal an open polynya in the area, and the most recent team visit to the Cape report that the land-based colony is recovering. For me, like Ransome's *Winter Holiday* youngsters, the ice created the means to an end. Another island ticked off that bucket-list.

Norfolk Island, 2001:

Situated in a no-man's patch of the North Tasman Sea, Norfolk has little attraction to the average sensible yachtee. It falls well wide of the rhumb from either New Zealand or Australia to any attractive Pacific destination. In fact, there is little to interest any self-respecting voyager, unless you count a handful of open roadstead anchorages which provide a potential lee for repairs.

Our passage from Sydney to Noumea had included a brief look-around at Lord Howe (a much more sensible stop-over with its reef-bounded lagoon). But the Nor-westerly was continuing to push us steadily further eastward from the rhumb until we realised that Norfolk was almost in our path. Rather conveniently, Babs had two first-cousins residing on the island at the time, one of whom had married into money, and as a result had recently purchased four duty-free shops as well as nearly half of the island's accommodation facilities. Popping in for a visit would be the right sort of family thing to do in the circumstances, so we consulted the chart and dropped our CQR in 23 metres onto a rocky bottom within a lumpy dinghy-ride distance from Kingston's historic stone pier. We were very aware that the freshening nor-westerly was likely heralding a sou'westerly front within the coming 24 hours, and the rock-holding may not be good enough for an on-shore windshift, so this would likely be a brief and somewhat edgy visit.

While we waited for a response from our VHF call to an unknown voice, enquiring whether Carol or her sister Robyn might be somehow contactable, we pored over the chart where the island's grim history as a penal colony was clearly evident in the names of the adjacent Slaughter Bay and Cemetery Bay. The subsequent relocation of Pitcairn Islanders here was also evident in various references to 'Bounty' and 'Fletcher's Mutiny'. From our vantage point, rolling uncomfortably in the wrap-around swell, Kingston appeared to be little more than a village, its handful of shops serving as a social focus for the island's two thousand inhabitants.

After thirty minutes with no VHF response, we were suddenly startled by the noise of a powerful outboard and a hail from a familiar female voice. Cousin Carol had wasted no time pulling in favours, and was already drawing alongside a smallish fishing charter boat. She was set to whisk us all ashore, with the (rather obvious) proviso that it would be unwise to leave our ketch unattended for more than an hour or two. Our concerns regarding a safe return were brushed aside with a convincing promise that the means were absolutely available to ensure that there would be no dramas - regardless of weather conditions which may eventuate.

It is a surreal experience being abruptly drawn back into the civilised world while still in a voyaging mindset. My brief drive around the island before returning aboard in our twelve-foot plywood dinghy was certainly fascinating, but for Babs the experience was even more bizarre. Not only was she ordered to bring all the dirty linen ashore to be washed and dried by Cousin Carol's bevy of cleaning staff, but there was a compulsory visit to her four village shops with instructions that a variety of items must be selected, free of charge, before being allowed to leave.

By mid-afternoon the westerly swell was increasing and the tide had risen, but the implications were not immediately obvious as I responded to a VHF call to bring the dinghy to the stone pier. Babs looked somewhat startled as I gunned the outboard and bought the big tender alongside the scarily solid structure. This was a very different experience from the morning's more benign conditions. A shallow reef, which had earlier been acting as a partial breakwater, was now fully submerged, and a relentless train of breaking swells was marching down the side of the pier as I did my best to lie alongside. Even as Babs threw down bags of clean laundry and assorted mysterious parcels, seawater was spilling over the pitching dinghy's bow.

Words were not necessary. As she shook her head and waved me away, I gunned the outboard and headed for open water with bags and parcels sloshing about my feet. There is little reserve buoyancy in our big tender, and it was a close call as it rose to meet an alarmingly steep swell before we were past the shallow reef and into less disturbed water. To this day, that moment was the closest I have been to capsizing our twelve-footer, and Babs still talks of the horror she felt watching me rearing to meet the near vertical swell face.

While I heaved my soggy cargo aboard over the Maid's rolling bulwarks and bailed, Babs was quelling a near mutiny from our two teenage youngest sons who had just been invited to to a sleep-over party. The battle between hormones and common-sense was settled without acrimony once they had joined her at the pier and surveyed the deteriorating sea-conditions. Cousin Carol seemed unfazed however, and before long the now-familiar fishing charter boat was being towed along the pier on a tandem trailer to a gantry at the midpoint, where my crew of three were told to embark as it hung in the slings. It was a slick operation, she told me later. They hung for several minutes until the skipper deemed it suitable to drop in using a rapid remote control. Then a longer wait, holding position a few metres from the pier as another set of swells rolled through.

Clearly this skipper had done this before. Suddenly they were out into open water, pulling alongside our rolling ketch as if this was just another day at the office. Three relieved faces and a fourth cheerful grin looked up at me as I took the painter and watched them clamber aboard. The salt-sodden laundry was a non-issue in the scheme of things – it was certainly cleaner than it had been on our arrival, and I had already admired the coil of rope that Babs had been gifted at Carol's hardware store. Our VHF thank-yous and farewells were cheerful, and we were ready to sail ahead of the coming cold front.

Norfolk had a final trick up its sleeve though. Our faithful old CQR was stubbornly wedged into a rock crack 22 metres below us, and it took a gypsy-lock and big swell to break it out. Its badly bent stock was to remind us of our visit for months. Anchors don't set happily when they are shaped like bananas.

Beautemps Beaupre Atoll, 2000:

We all love deserted islands, especially our teenage sons who enjoy camping ashore to escape their Aged Parents. One of our favourites is in the Loyalty Islands. Most Pacific passage-makers consider Ouvea to be the northern-most in this chain, as it has facilities ashore. Also, any passage between New Caledonia and Vanuatu doesn't allow for customs clearance in the Loyalty group As a result the northernmost small uninhabited atoll of Beautemps Beaupre, with its substantial surrounding lagoon, is a little-visited gem.

We were cruising in company with a 60ft Tasmanian ketch, *Southern Cross* , when we decided to pay it a visit. Our boys had a thinly disguised urge to persuade their teenage daughter to camp ashore, which made the dynamics rather amusing.

The seven-mile-wide lagoon has an easy entrance a couple of miles north of the atoll, but anchoring so far from the lure of palm trees in accelerated trade winds was not particularly pleasant, especially as close inspection by dinghy showed a miniature sheltered lagoon in the lee of the island within swimming distance ashore. Between our ketches and this heavenly little potential anchorage was a hopeful belt of pale blue water.

Pale blue in the tropics depicts sand bottom, and a few quick soundings with our six-foot oars was sufficient to indicate that we could ease our 5 ft draft ketch across this sandbar with an inch or two to spare. Once in, though, the boys were like cats on hot bricks. What use was this snug anchorage when the object of their mutual desires was anchored a couple of miles to the north aboard a 7ft draft ketch?

Within an hour they had a solution. Close inspection by dinghy revealed a convoluted potential entry between coral-heads from the open sea to the south-west. All that would be needed were half a dozen weights and floats to mark the zigzag channel. Contact was made, and by evening both ketches swung peacefully in a quiet haven while some exuberant teenagers were setting up camp ashore.

Our ten-day stay had its moments. The youngsters' amorous adventure was swiftly curtailed when it was discovered that our boys had crafted a pair of coconut-shell bras with the expectation that their fourteen-year-old campmate would model for them. The boys were appropriately recalled to complete some overdue school assignments, and camping was struck off the list for the Tasmanian children, replaced by the less questionable activities of raft-building and snorkling.

The only other vessel to briefly drop anchor in the lagoon was an American sloop with a powerful HF radio, whose skipper was pleasantly prepared to relay our boys' correspondence-school exam results via a series of phone connections in New Zealand. However a slightly more intrusive visit came from overhead, when the New Caledonian customs helicopter buzzed in to check the anchorage for undesirables. Our personal relationship with French authorities was a tenuous one, having spent considerable time protesting against their nuclear tests in the Tuamotos five years earlier. Two uniformed men beckoned from the beach, and our Tasmanian fellow-skipper hastened ashore from the big ketch to assure these officials that he was of a more respectable calibre than those Kiwis out there. He returned with his tail between his legs however, after learning that it was his vessel they were looking for, not ours, as his cruising permit was due to expire in four days' time. He had been sternly instructed to return to Noumea immediately, before the chopper flew off without a backward glance at our black former protest vessel.

Their visit precipitated a departure which was already inevitable, as we were now eking out the drinking water from the big ketch's rusty reserve tank, and had run out of coke for the rum. Our final evening's beach barbecue was moistened with a blend of coconut juice and rum (of which we still had plenty), while the youngsters placed their weighted floats to mark our outbound reef pass. The cheerful waves from the girl's parents may have belied a tinge of relief as we parted company. Hormones can generate complications in teenage-hood, especially on deserted islands.

*Snorkling alongside **Southern Cross** was a less questionable activity.*

AUTHOR'S NOTE:

There have been so many fascinating encounters during our cruising decades that I decided to blend them into semi-fictional children's novels.

The following piece about a small-boat misadventure has been adapted from ***Those Sugar-Barge Kids*** – the fourth title in a series that I wrote as a reflection of the lifestyle that our sons and grandkids have enjoyed. Any reader familiar with Arthur Ransome's ***Swallows and Amazons*** may notice an element of the 'Battle for Houseboat Bay' in this piece, although the context and outcome are rather different from the two lug-rigged pirate dinghies which stormed Captain Flint's black houseboat!

The huge old barge originally carried sugar across Auckland Harbour before the bridge was built. This barge has in real life been home to two generations of youngsters, nestled among the mangroves in a northern New Zealand inlet. We originally met two of them, happily fending for themselves while their solo father was away for a few days.

*David Bamford's lovely old ketch was already named **Swallow** when he bought her and restored her. He has been a fan of Arthur Ransome's **Swallows and Amazons** book series for many years.*

16

Range and Trajectory

The mood was cheerful as the older three children rowed the red Seabird dinghy through the narrow channel between sprawling mangrove trees toward the old sugar-barge. Ella seemed lost in thought. "Did you say there was a black two-master anchored at the island?"

Jake nodded. "Fin and I saw it from the top of your hill."

"That'll be Captain Bamford's *Swallow*. He anchors there a lot." A mischievous grin lit up Ella's face. "We've got plenty of time to get there and back before half tide. That's over three hours away. We can come back up the main channel. It's deeper." She pointed out through the gap in the mangroves toward open water, then turned her head towards the south channel to yell to her sister. "HURRY UP SAM!" They could barely see the green Heron dinghy moving lazily towards them through the tangle of branches and leaves. "We'd better get some stuff quickly. Come on." Flicking the painter over a cleat on the floating jetty, she ran to the steps and bounded up to the deck-house door ahead of Jess. "Grab some bread and stuff for lunch – anything'll do. Knife and breadboard too. Maybe some pears. I'll be back in a jiff."

The old sugar-barge, nestled between sprawling mangrove trees.

A moment later she was back with a bulging sack. "We need the fresh battery too. You're strong Jake. It's in the locker behind the deckhouse. You can lug it down to *Death 'n Glory* as soon as those two slow-coaches tie up." She turned away and cupped her hands around her mouth. "HURRY UP SAM - WE'RE GOING TO THE ISLAND NOW."

There was barely time for a drink and a visit to the ship's head before the green dinghy pulled up alongside the red Seabird. Sam and Fin seemed excited at the prospect of a two-dinghy expedition to the island. While they took turns to visit the barge's composting toilet, the older three kids busied themselves wiping some of the mud out of *Jolly Roger*, and switching *Death 'n Glory's* heavy flat battery for Jake's charged one.

"We won't sail there. You'll see why soon," said Ella mysteriously. "We'll tow you with the electric outboard. The wind's in the west now but at least the tide's in our favour. What say we let Sam and Fin go in your red dinghy, and we can tow them in *Death 'n Glory*." It was a popular suggestion, and moments later they were moving sedately out into the inlet.

At first the wind and current were both helping them along, but as soon as they were around the headland the breeze was in their faces, and the outboard had a slightly higher-pitched hum. Ella pointed at the black ketch anchored a mile away near the island's southern beach, and turned her head to call back to Sam. "I don't think he's seen us - can't see him on deck. But his flag's flying." She steered along the coastline northwards until the yacht was out of sight behind the still-distant island, then altered course directly towards the beach on the island's northern side.

It was obvious to Jake, looking at her secretive smile, that she was planning some mischief. The dinghies bounced and splashed their way against small choppy waves, and when Jake suggested that maybe they would go faster if he rowed to help the outboard, Ella nodded. This definitely made a difference, and before long Fin and Sam were rowing in the red dinghy behind them too, rather jerkily with an oar each, still under tow with the mast and rolled-up sail between them.

As well as helping their speed, the rowing made time pass more quickly. It didn't take much effort with the motor doing most of the work. Jess took one of Jake's oars and rowed next to him for a while until Ella decided to swap with her. Occasionally they paused to bale out some of the water that was splashing over their starboard bow. Jake was beginning to wish he had brought a waterproof jacket. The whole back and left side of his sweatshirt were becoming quite wet under his lifejacket. It was a relief to reach sheltered water close to the beach.

Ella was back in the stern by now. The humming noise stopped as she twisted the tiller controls and tilted the propeller clear of the water. She cast off the towrope, and a moment later they crunched up onto crushed shells and sand, with the red dinghy veering away to miss them. "Tide's falling fast, but we'll still tie to those trees in case there's a surge," she instructed to nobody in particular. She seemed more interested in wading out with her bulging sack and dunking it several times in the water.

Sam glanced across at her, with a broad grin, as she tied *Jolly Roger*'s painter to the same tree that Jake had just used for *Death'n Glory*. "I don't think he saw us," she called. "How many did you get?" Ella held up four fingers. Sam did a little skip of excitement. "Come on you guys - yeah just chuck your lifejackets in our boat. Let's go." She led off up a steep overgrown track.

Jake brought up the rear, carrying Ella's dripping sack. It was surprisingly heavy, and he was puffing when he joined the other four in a trampled clearing at the top of a long ridge. Both of the sugar-barge girls were peering excitedly through a gap in the trees as Jake dumped the sack on the ground. The three Tasmanian children crowded around them to look down at the old black ketch anchored close to the other beach. A large red flag flapped at its mizzen masthead, with a white skull and crossed swords clearly visible in the steady breeze.

"He's definitely hoping we'll come, and he's anchored in range," crowed Ella, emptying the sack onto the ground. Four cabbage-sized balls of seaweed tumbled out, trussed up with windings of twine and oozing muddy seawater. "We'll get him totally by surprise," she giggled.

Jake was already eying a pair of thin lines strung between two trees, with a large bowl hanging between them over an old wooden tent-peg. Two pairs of holes had been drilled near the rim opposite each other, with the parallel cords threaded into each side. Jess joined him, fingering the cord with curiosity. "It's bungee cord. Look." She pulled it back and released it with a twang.

Jake realised with a sudden flash, what this was. "Hey Ella, Sam - it's a giant catapult, isn't it?" He pulled the bowl back, stretching the bungee, then released it. The bowl flew through the air, fetching up abruptly and pinging back towards him. He jumped aside hurriedly. "This is awesome! Do you fire those seaweed things like cannonballs?"

Sam was about to speak when Ella beat her to it. "We've worked out the trajectories using basic trigonometry. Get the range sticks Sam."

Sam knelt to pull two sticks from under a bush and a length of thin rope. One was forked, with thin black cords tied across it like strings on a harp. The other was long and straight with notches carved into it at regular intervals. She passed the straight stick and rope to Ella, and put the forked stick on her shoulder, bending slightly as she squinted through the strings towards the black boat. "Third string Ella."

"It's a giant catapult, isn't it !"

Her older sister frowned with concentration briefly. "That's forty-five metres." She looked up to her fascinated friends. "She was just finding the angle between *Swallow* and that log on the beach, to tell how far out he's anchored. We calibrated it ages ago. Now for the elevation – this is a bit of guesswork coz the mud-bombs aren't all the same weight. We just work from the average ..."

"...three kilos is what they usually are, depending on how long we wet them for," finished Sam.

"We have to pull the bungee cords back for the same amount of stretch each time," continued Ella, dropping a loop over a greying tent-peg below the drooping bowl, and walking backwards until the rope was stretched straight, pointing towards the black ketch.

"So that's what that wooden peg was for," murmured Jake. He had no idea that this was going to be such a precise exercise. He watched as Ella poked the long stick into the ground at the end of the rope.

She pushed and wriggled it until one of the notches was just buried. "Forty-five metres is the second notch from the top."

"I thought it was the third," interrupted Sam. "Okay, okay – have it your way."

Fin was already holding a dripping mud-bomb, eager to load it into the bowl. Ella nodded for him to bring it. "Sometimes I think Captain Bamford anchors close like this to make it easy."

It was a long way to stretch the bungy. Sam and Ella had clearly done this before, pulling back evenly until they reached the notched stick, then lowering the bowl until the lower lip was in line with the second notch from the top. "Two, six, FIRE!" With a twang the bowl shot forward in a shower of muddy spray, and the weedy missile soared upwards. The girls sprang sideways to catch the bungy, as their three Tasmanian friends crowded closer for a view.

It was a remarkably near miss, landing with a splash just short of the black hull towards the bow. "Okay Sam – third notch this time and slightly to the right." Jake noticed a white-bearded face appear through the aft hatch and look around. The girls ducked. "Down everybody. He'll probably think it was a gannet." She peered through the leaves. "Okay he's gone back down."

The second shot was almost perfect. It hit the mizzen-mast with a glancing blow, bursting open with a shower of mud. This time a head and shoulders appeared, looked up, then across at the island, shook his fist and disappeared quickly below again.

"Quick Fin – one more. Third notch again Sam. Two, six, FIRE!" The old man had just climbed into the cockpit with a long object that looked distinctly like an old musket, and was poking something red into it when the third mud-bomb exploded onto the cabin-top. He turned directly towards their clearing, shaking his fist and pointing the musket towards them.

It was too far to tell clearly, but Jake thought he could see a broad smile on the old man's face. There was a puff of smoke from the musket, followed instantly by a loud bang.

Fin jumped back in alarm. "He's firing at us! Get down!" Ella grinned at him, scooping the last mud-bomb back into her sack.

"It's okay Fin. Now we've got to finish the raid. It'll be much better now we've got two boats. You'll need your pirate flag too."

*

Back down on the island's northern beach again, minutes after the old captain had fired his musket, there was plenty of activity as both dinghy crews prepared for a boarding party onto his black ketch. Masts were stepped - with the boat-hook pirate flag re-attached to *Jolly Roger*'s mast-head - and the sails made ready.

Ella issued instructions as they busied themselves "We'll tack upwind around the western end so we can run downwind to *Swallow*. That'll give him less time to see us coming. We can both sail down outside him. You three can round up and board him on his port side and we'll sail around his stern and climb aboard on his starboard side. He won't have a chance."

Jake was torn between the excitement of the raid and the practical problems of dealing with flapping sails and choppy waters alongside the larger yacht. "We can't all just jump aboard and abandon the dinghies, Ella. We'll have to drop the sails and then maybe let them drift astern."

Ella looked startled. Jake guessed that she was used to issuing orders, not having discussions about her plans. "Mmmm … okay, maybe someone will have to stay in the dinghies and fend off. He's a bit fussy about his paintwork."

Jess nodded quickly. "I don't mind looking after *Jolly Roger*. I can pull the mast out with the sail still on it – we've done that lots of times. We can add some rope to the painter so that she'll drift a long way clear."

Jake was thinking out loud. "Maybe Fin can go in *Death'n Glory* with you two. He could pull down your jib as soon as you ease sheets at the top of the island – you won't need it downwind. And it would be better if you and Sam lead the raid – you're Captain Bamford's friends and he doesn't know us. Fin knows how to drop your mains'l and fend off." He watched Fin's face as he spoke. As expected, there was a flash of disappointment, followed by a slightly grudging nod.

"Have you done this before?" Jess was beginning to wonder if Ella really knew what she was doing, despite her bossy instructions.

Ella looked at Sam briefly and nodded vaguely. "Yep. Twice. The first time we sneaked up under oars and caught him by total surprise."

"It was calm though," added Sam. "But the second time he knew we were coming coz we'd splattered him, and he pushed us both into the water."

"Okay, but have you sailed alongside *Swallow* on a day like this?" From the look on Ella and Sam's faces, it was clear that this was going to be a new experience.

Jake spoke quickly, not wanting to spoil the raid. "It's a great plan Ella – we should do it like you say, but maybe us boys will take care of the dinghies and you three girls can lead the boarding party. We'll join you when we've dumped the sails and tied them astern. But what exactly are you going to do to him? He seemed pretty old."

Ella laughed. "Yep, but he reckons the occasional sea-battle helps make him feel young again. He'll try to push you in – can you swim?" They all nodded vigorously. "We try to tie him up and hoist our flag – oops, I left it behind. We'll hoist yours instead." She paused and looked at them all. "Better not be too rough though - don't want anyone hurt.

THE MOMENT THEY rounded the western end of the island they could see the old captain in his cockpit scanning the other end of the island with a telescope. He turned towards the bow and looked their way just as Fin finished pulling down the jib on the green dinghy. They were close enough to see the surprise on his face at the sight of not one but *two* small pirate vessels sweeping rapidly downwind towards his ketch.

Jake was concentrating on leaving enough room for Ella to steer between *Jolly Roger* and *Swallow* when he heard a sharp bang. *Death'n Glory* was already nearly a dinghy-length ahead, which suited their plans, and as he looked sharply across

Fin finished pulling down the jib ...

behind her stern he saw the old captain lower his musket and drop a red object into its barrel. "Watch where you're steering!" hissed Jess, and he pushed the tiller to straighten up.

Jake glanced ahead at Ella who was clearly watching the musket more than her sails or her steering. A second later, just as her green Heron swept past *Swallow*'s stern, the black sail crashed across in a sudden gybe. At the same instant there was another bang and flash from the musket – then *Death'n Glory* was on her side, black sail floating on the water, and three heads bobbing among the little choppy waves. Jake had practised capsizing his Optimist dinghy plenty of times, and something didn't seem right as he stared, horrified. The green dinghy was deeper in the water than it should be.

"I'm gybing Jess," he almost shouted at his sister, even though she was close enough to touch. She ducked instantly and rolled across to port, letting the mainsheet run free as the sail slammed over. Jake straightened the tiller and rounded up into the wind as close as possible to the black hull. A worried-looking white-bearded face was staring down at him, then at Jess, then back.

"Sorry Captain Bamford - can you take the painter - this is Jess - I gotta go – sorry." It wasn't the way he liked to meet people, but this wasn't a normal situation. He scrambled aboard and raced across to the other side-deck. *Death'n Glory* was even lower in the water now, and moving slowly past as the ebb current carried her past *Swallow*'s starboard side against the wind. Fin and Sam were clutching the mast, while Ella was trying swim her way around the transom towards the centreboard.

Jake took a deep breath and jumped, landing in the murky choppy water with a splash near Ella, and feeling the buoyancy of his lifejacket pulling him upwards until his head and shoulders were clear of the water. Salt water filled his nose and mouth – a bitter taste which reminded him of his own capsizes back home in Tasmania. The cold water was already seeping through his shirt, and his eyes stung as he looked toward Ella.

She spoke in short panicky breaths. "The battery Jake – it's sinking the boat. I think the locker's leaking."

Jake had forgotten about that heavy battery. It must be dragging the boat down. Trying to stand on the centreboard like he did on his own Optimist, *Privateer*, might make the locker fill faster. "Wait Ella! Hey Fin, Sam, can you find the painter – I need it. Quick!" Out of the corner of his eye he saw the white beard again and called up: "Can you chuck me a line – before they drift too far?"

Captain Bamford definitely knew how to throw a rope properly – the coiled end landed with a splash right next to Jake's arm. Fin was already swimming towards him with the end of the painter while Sam tried to stop the mast from going underwater. Jake fumbled as he tied the rope to the painter, starting with a sheet bend then changing his mind and tying a reef knot with extra hitches for luck.

Jess was on deck now too, helping pull the capsized pirate dinghy closer. Once they had reached his knot he knew what needed doing next. "I'm gonna dive for the battery." He was already slipping out of his lifejacket. "Can you mind this for me Ella?" Looking up at Jess's anxious face, he added: "I need that rope again now. I'll be fine. I'll just tie it around the battery handle and come back up for air. Maybe you can pull the dinghy close to the bowsprit so you and the captain can drag the battery up from there - then we can get their dinghy righted aga..." A wave slopped into his mouth and he spluttered, gulping seawater. Without his lifejacket it was harder work, treading water and messing with ropes.

Ella's face, bobbing higher in the water near his, was full of mixed emotions – self-blame and gratitude mixed with a slight hint of jealousy. "Hold onto this till you're ready to dive," she ordered, thrusting his lifejacket back at him. "Swim round the other side and I'll flick the rope over to you. It should be me diving – but ...." She looked away for a few seconds, embarrassed.

Jake was already swimming, hugging his lifejacket to his chest with one arm and paddling with the other. "Don't worry," he called back over his shoulder, accidentally gulping another mouthful of seawater. "I've done this before." Deep down, he wasn't quite as confident as he sounded. During his Optimist sailing course in Tasmania, he once had to swim under the upturned dinghy and breathe the air that had been trapped inside. But this would be a deeper dive, in murky water with no air to breathe.

After working his way around, pulling past the rudder, he had to wriggle between the boom and the hull to reach the place where the middle seat should be, alongside the centre-case. He tossed his lifejacket to Fin and tried to remember where he had stowed the battery before they left the sugar-barge. Under the seat next to the long centre-case – was it to port or starboard? Hopefully to port or else it would have slid right down to the deepest part of the dinghy.

Something brushed past his head – the end of the rope. Grasping it firmly and taking a deep breath, he dived, pulling himself down on the mainsheet and feeling around until he found the seat. There – he could feel something. It was definitely the battery lodged against the centre-case, lying on its side. He fumbled for its handle to tie a knot, but his lungs were already bursting. He shoved the rope through the handle and swam upwards with the end, briefly panicking to find his head under the black sail. Luckily his head was close enough to the boom to force his way out into clear water, and he grabbed at the gunwale, gasping for air.

"Found it!" His eyes were stinging from the seawater, but he could see that the dinghy had already been pulled much closer to Swallow's bowsprit. Two blurry faces were looking down at him. "I'll tie a bowline here. Then can you pull from up there? We've got to get it out of the dinghy."

It was harder than expected. With the painter tied to Swallow's fore-deck bollard, the capsized dinghy had been swivelled by the current until it was lying bow-to-bow with the ketch. Fin and Sam were still doing a great job keeping the mast and sail on the surface, using Jake's lifejacket as a float.

Jake felt a tug on his arm. It was Ella. "I'll help. You okay?" Jake nodded. Above their heads, on Swallow's bowsprit, Jess and Captain

Bamford were already pulling on Jake's rope. *Death'n Glory* floated noticeably higher as they heaved. The rope was dragging on the mast's side-stay. It was Ella who noticed the battery snagging on the turnbuckle.

"Wait!" It was a struggle for them both to drag it clear of the rigging. They watched it swing across to bounce off *Swallow*'s bobstay, before being hauled up onto the foredeck. Jake was beginning to feel sick.

*

Twenty minutes later, everyone was on deck with both pirate dinghies tethered astern. Jake had been pleased that Ella took over the task of righting the green Heron. She had let go the halliard and pulled the black sail partly down before they had swum back around to stand on the centreboard together. The dinghy had rolled back upright easily enough, wallowing drunkenly in the choppy water. Fin and Sam had already begun bucketing out the water when he had climbed the rope ladder and been promptly sick.

Now, huddled together in *Swallow*'s mud-splattered cockpit shivering slightly, four soggy young would-be pirates and one dry one were noisily chattering with the elderly retired pirate, while they munched cheerfully on handfuls of chocolate and nuts while both pirate dinghies bobbed astern. There was plenty to talk about. Captain Bamford had already learned their names even before Fin and Sam had dripped their way up the rope ladder, and seemed genuinely pleased to have so much chatter around him, now that the capsize drama was over. He chuckled when Fin immediately began pestering him to look at the musket.

"I hope you can keep a secret," he whispered loudly with a wink. "My reputation as a fearsome pirate is at stake here." He lifted the antique-looking weapon from inside the companionway hatch and handed it to Fin.

"It's light – really light." Fin balanced it on the palm of one hand.

"It came from a film set that I was involved in once – actually a fibreglass replica." He rummaged in his pocket, pulling out a large red firecracker and cigarette lighter. "Works like this." He lit the fuse and dropped the cracker down the barrel, quickly pointing it into the air. The sharp crack that followed made them all jump, even though they were expecting it. "Works perfectly as a distraction. I didn't expect to sink your ship quite so easily though!" He looked at Ella and chuckled again. "Next time I'll enlist Jake here as my crew. He can dive for any treasure in a sinking ship."

"Were you really a pirate once?" asked Fin.

"Definitely – well … of a sort. Have you ever heard of the pirate radio station ship in the Hauraki Gulf, years ago? I worked aboard that for a while. The police tried to stop us leaving Auckland harbour, then our first ship was wrecked, and we had to put out a mayday over the top of the music."

They were warming up now, and once the captain's chocolate and nuts had disappeared, Jess produced the loaf of bread and some honey that she had packed in haste back at the sugar-barge. Between mouthfuls Jake quizzed Ella about the capsize. She had barely opened her mouth to speak when Sam drowned her out.

The old retired pirate chuckled.

"I got the mainsheet tangled in my legs. Ella didn't tell us she was gybing. We were watching the musket. I got thrown on top of the sail, but Fin stopped us from going right upside down."

"Dad made us practise gybing before we were allowed to sail to the island last year," added Ella more quietly. "But we didn't have the battery then. Also I didn't screw the lid back on the starboard buoyancy locker this morning. Please don't tell Dad. Do you think the battery's okay?" Jake studied her face as she spoke. She seemed somehow different from the bossy girl he had first met barely a day ago. Perhaps this capsize had knocked her confidence. He was about to speak when the old captain beat him to it.

"The battery should be fine Ella. It's a sealed unit. Just give it a good charge-up when you get home."

Jess was quick to add some words of encouragement too. "We've all capsized before, Ella. It's good experience really ..."

"... and *Death'n Glory* isn't damaged or anything either," interrupted Jake. "It made the battle more exciting." He looked up at the mud-splattered mizzen mast, and then at the captain. "They hit our mast with one of those things yesterday too, when we were sailing past. It's an amazing catapult."

Ella stooped to peer through the hatch at *Swallow*'s clock. "Is that the time? We've only got an hour to get back or we'll miss the tide. And there's heaps of scrubbing to do. We'll all have to do it." She stood up. "Sam, you and Fin can scrub that mud off the cabin-top. Jake you're strong – you can fill up the buckets for us. Jess and I can scrub the mizzen and cockpit." Jake couldn't hide his grin. Ella was back to her old bossy self again.

*

IT'S SURPRISING HOW quickly five kids can clean up a mud-spattered boat when they have a tide to beat. Twenty minutes later the old captain emerged for the inspection, to find *Swallow* very nearly as spick and span as she had been before this horde of young pirates had fired their volley of mudballs. Pretending to grumble, he carried up a tiny sea-chest, and opened it. Jake peered over Sam's shoulder to see it half filled with dozens of small gold coins. For a moment he thought they were two-dollar coins, until he remembered that in New Zealand the smallest gold coins are the one-dollar ones.

Captain Bamford counted out ten coins into Ella's hand, then looked at Sam. "Two hits, so I guess that's another ten dollars," he said, counting ten into her outstretched hand. "I hope you two are going to put this ill-gotten money to good use, and don't forget that these friends of yours did more than half of the clean-up."

They were grateful to have the westerly breeze that had caused so much trouble. As the two dinghies surged their way back up the inlet, Jake grinned across at Ella, only half a dinghy-length ahead, and she smiled back sheepishly.

***

17

Just Another Shopping Trip.

As I write, with my back to a bulkhead and the glow of a little woodstove barely a metre from my left hip, I'm reflecting on my teenage decision to build a home that would float. A black one with a pair of masts. And true to my dream, since we moved aboard over three decades ago, *New Zealand Maid* has been our only home, except for a two-year interlude when we built ourselves a bush-block solar house on a Tasmanian island.

Living aboard is not the romantic lifestyle that some might imagine. But nor is it a miserable existence. Put simply, we liveaboards are atune to a richly different set of everyday challenges than a suburban dweller. And the rewards are certainly satisfying.

Three days ago, Babs and I sat down to plan a shopping day from our current mooring in northern New Zealand's Bay of Islands. Such occasions are dictated to by factors irrelevant to house-based urbanites. The brass clock on the bulkhead behind me is more than just a timepiece. In addition to its three conventional hands, it has a fourth blue hand, which reveals the state of tide. These tides are vitally important to our existence and planning. During last night for example, I glanced at this clock in the red glow of a night-light as I groggily passed it on my way to deal with a persistent thumping near our windvane astern. The clock confirmed what I already suspected – it was 0430 hrs, and the tide had turned. The dinghy which I had streamed astern during the ebb after dark was now being pinned to the counter-stern by the incoming current, while the *Maid* was still lying head to wind. In dirty easterly weather like this, it was time to tether our 12 ft tender alongside and bail it out, if I was to get any sleep during the remaining hours of darkness.

This latest fortnightly shopping trip was to purchase various perishable provisions and a few vulnerable items which would need to stay dry. We like to stay dry too of course, which is where the weather comes in. I would like to boast that we tap our barometer daily, hold up our licked fingers to test the breeze, and scan the sky for mares' tails and mackerel scales. Certainly during our first decade afloat, such eyeball weather-forecasting was vital, supplemented only by the single 0530hr daily marine forecast from our AM transistor radio. But to be truthful we have moved with the times like any sensible sailor. At sea we pore over the MSL faxes downloaded from HF radio to a laptop. And near land (as we currently are) our mobile devices have multiple weather apps which provide us with up to ten days of predictions from the Meteorology Bureau, as well as more detailed predictions for a week ahead, from four independent weather models.

Babs is fixated on weather. She is also a pessimist, while I'm an optimist. She tends to seek out the most unpleasant model while I focus on most hopeful. Usually we arrive at a compromise. For the shopping trip we were planning, the predictions were not looking good. The most likely scenario for the morrow showed easterly winds of 25 knots gusting 35, followed by gales, heavy falls of rain and possible thunderstorms persisting during the following days. Delays were not an option as we were nearly out of potatoes and wine.

Our current base, between regular coastal forays, is a mooring in far-north New Zealand. Getting to the dinghy dock requires us to cross an inlet in our wooden 12ft 'longboat', and continue for a nautical mile through a field of moored boats in a separate estuary. Currents flow in and out of each waterway, so we have a convergence to cross along the way. The fetch for our

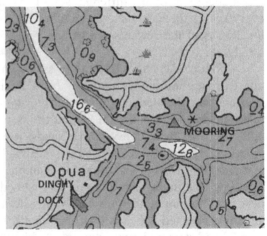

inlet in an easterly is about eight miles, so the wind-chop waves are a significant factor in our planning. The best time to return aboard will be at slack water or at least when wind is not against tide. A lesser factor during these easterlies are the swells which wrap around several headlands and counter-intuitively roll gently into our inlet from the northwest against the wind. This meant, for our planning, we would bolt on the outboard motor, rather than rely on four-oar-power to get ashore. We would need a conservative four-hour allowance to get to the nearest city (Whangarei) carry out our various chores, and return aboard.

It was a potentially fraught operation, lowering a 23kg outboard motor onto the transom of a prancing dinghy tethered alongside, so once again the blue hand on our clock was helpful, as was the tide app on my phone. High tide would be at about 0900. This would be the best time to transfer the outboard, with the *Maid* providing a lee for the dinghy as she swung during the slack. Then, if we made our move ashore before the tide began to ebb too hard, the wind would be with tide, and we wouldn't have too much current against us in the mooring field. There might still be the odd whitecap splashing aboard if we crossed the inlet beam-on to the waves, so our strategy would involve taking them on our quarter until the estuary provided a lee.

Before we set off that morning in the steady rain, there were waterproof bags to collect, along with a blue tarp and our full wet-weather gear. Wallets and phones needed to be bundled into a dry bag before we set off. Then a quick check of the mooring line and a start-up of the outboard while Babs was still up on deck. The agreed drill is generally for me to let go the dinghy stern-line before climbing down, while Babs is responsible for the painter until the outboard is warmed up.

We consider ourselves fortunate to be based in this location at present. The dinghy dock is a floating pontoon, unlike many cat-walk jetties we have experienced in harbours with big tidal ranges (or worse still, a beach involving tedious dragging). There is no ladder to be climbed here, just a ramp and, if we are lucky, maybe even a trolley within a few minutes' walk from the dock when we return from town.

Once ashore alongside our trusty old van, all that remained was to strip off our sodden wet-weather gear and bundle it into the boot, before transforming our mindsets into the world of the landlubber. It takes contrasting experiences to savour the easy bits in life, and for us the luxury of vehicle transport is something we probably appreciate more than most regular shoppers.

In our post-covid world, shopping still has challenges which most landlubbers will understand, so there is little need to dwell on these, except that in our case the self-imposed deadline required a return shortly before slack low water. Our real world returned as we descended the hill towards the dock, pulling over briefly to assess the whitecaps and the intervals between squalls. This done, it was time to find somewhere to park within easy walking distance from the dock.

Our fortnight's worth of provisions and extras amounted to several shopping bags, some quite heavy. After donning soggy wet weather gear and seeking out a trolley, these bags needed to be cocooned in a blue tarp and manoeuvred down the slippery now-steep ramp to the floating dock where our waterlogged dinghy awaited. There is little need to describe the strategy of our return trip between squalls. As before, it entailed stowing cargo amidships and making use of whatever lee and lulls that were available.

Anyone who has brought a dinghy alongside a larger vessel in a seaway will know about the nuisance little wave-slops that squirt between hulls at four-second intervals. These were our final challenge, so the exercise of stemming the current, timing the leap aboard, making the painter fast and transferring our somewhat damp cargo aboard was simply a part of our regular life, perfectly unremarkable.

However, when we next notice the wine-locker becoming depleted, I have the feeling that we will pay rather more attention to those weather models a few days ahead. Going shopping on a calm day may be anti-climatic, but it does add a layer of pleasure to remind us how wonderful it is to live afloat. So on the subject of contentment, perhaps we could offer *you* a little advice? Well-intentioned, of course !

***

MORE BOOKS BY JON TUCKER

A TRUE SAILING CLASSIC (SOLD IN 37 COUNTRIES)

When Ben Tucker and his kid brother Matt decided to sail south looking for icebergs in Ben's small home-built kiwi yacht, they allowed their father to come as their cabin-boy, on his promise of good behaviour.

The unfolding adventure took them through thick pack ice to become trapped at the *windiest location on the planet,* a remote location in East Antarctica.

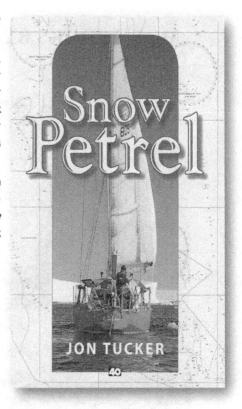

"An extraordinary tale of sailing — well outside the genre of most sailing books."

(Dr Nick Gales— Director, Australian Antarctic Division)

"...an exceptional work by a gifted writer.

So compelling that one wishes it not to end."

(Janet Upcher-reviewer)

"...a textured, intriguing, exhilarating story."

(Rachel Edwards—book show host)

"...up there with the best. Jon's writing style is perfect."

(Don McIntyre—adventurer/columnist)

'Those Kids' series

This linked series of stand-alone books follow the adventures of three home-schooled sailing children in Australia and New Zealand during the course of a two year Pacific voyage.

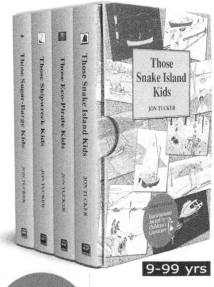

Eight-year-old Anna Willoughby's delighted face says it all, after she has collected more books in this series for her parents to read to her.

I am writing to say that I absolutely LOVE Jon Tucker's 'Those Kids' book series. His books are easy-going reading, with intriguing plot ideas and fun, unique, detailed, characters. They are wonderful, and they keep me so entertained! In fact, I think I have read each of them at least 5 times!

May Kelly, Grade Six, Riverhead School

Acclaimed by numerous readers of all ages throughout the English-speaking world, this series has proven appeal on many levels.

The reader learns not just sailing skills but also life skills... And underlying all of this is a real sense that the author has genuine warmth for children and understands and advocates for the importance of children's adventuring.

One young reader I spoke to said, "I love the way the story focuses on environmental issues, like plastic rubbish in the oceans. These issues are real for us and these books inspire me to be part of the solution."

Cathy Catton -reviewer, Practical Boat Owner magazine

Recommended by the Children's Book Councils of Australia and New Zealand.